THE **WORLD SAUCES** COOKBOOK

THE WORLD SAUCES COOKBOOK | MARK C. STEVENS

60 Regional Recipes and 30 Perfect Pairings

FOREWORD BY SUSAN PUCKETT
Photography by Nadine Greeff

ROCKRIDGE
PRESS

Interior and Cover Designer: Joshua Moore
Art Producer: Karen Beard
Editor: Kim Suarez, Daniel Grogan
Production Editor: Andrew Yackira
Photography © 2019 Nadine Greeff. Author photo courtesy of © Jess Kearney
Cover Recipes (left to right): Mango Chutney, page 12; "Catch-All" Barbecue Sauce, page 42; Sauvignon Blanc Cream Sauce, page 34

ISBN: Print 978-1-64152-478-0 | eBook 978-1-64152-479-7

This book is dedicated to all those who, without question, open their kitchens to voyagers from distant lands. And to my mom, who carried me on her hip across the sea before I could walk.

Questo libro è dedicato a coloro che, senza chiedere nulla in cambio, aprono la loro casa a quelli che vengono da lontano. E a mia mamma, che mi ha portato in braccio attraverso terre e mari prima ancora che imparassi a camminare da solo.

Contents

Foreword

N THE SUMMER OF 2018, I CAME BACK TO MY HOMETOWN OF
Jackson, Mississippi, to appear on a panel with several other cookbook
authors at the Mississippi Book Festival and talk about storytelling by
way of food. Three of us were Mississippi natives with books primarily
focused on the flavors closest to our Southern hearts. The fourth
panelist, Mark C. Stevens, came with a different perspective.

A nomad of sorts who works in the film industry when he's not trotting
the globe, he'd just had his first cookbook published: *Cooking with Spices:
100 Recipes for Blends, Marinades, and Sauces from Around the World*. To say
he took the research seriously is an understatement. Aside from studying the
origins of each seasoning on his laptop, he traveled straight to several of the
sources on every continent, tasting the most authentic dishes of each spot he
visited and chatting up the local cooks who made them.

As I listened to him speak about the lessons he'd learned—from watching
his Italian Nonna prepare pesto alla Genovese in the Mediterranean coastal
town of Chiavari, to getting schooled in the art of seasoning fresh meat over
a *parrilla* flame in Argentina—it became clear to me why he'd been invited to
join this discussion. Southerners love swapping stories as much as they do
sharing their favorite foods with friends and strangers alike, and Mark fit right
in. The crowd of food-loving Mississippi folks was clearly charmed.

Happily, the conversation didn't end after the Q&A. We ended up hanging
out together much of the rest of the weekend, sampling the traditional and
uptown cuisine of some of the local restaurants, listening to live music at a
popular downtown bar, and yapping endlessly about dining adventures at
home and abroad. We parted ways with vows to keep in touch, and we have.

I've continued to follow his culinary escapades on Instagram. Should he ever start leading food tours, I'll be ready to sign up. I was especially delighted to hear that he was working on a follow-up to his excellent *Cooking with Spices* with a global guide to sauces, and honored to get a sneak peek.

Like the seasoning blends of his first book, these recipes have backstories that open windows into other cultures. They're also easy and practical to execute no matter where you live, and enormously versatile. Blend a selection of red and green chiles with shrimp paste and a few pantry staples, and you have an insider's version of the fiery Indonesian sauce known as Sambel Ulek (page 30) to jazz up a plain pan-seared chicken thigh or a sautéed pork chop. Glaze a grilled salmon steak or a bison burger with Huckleberry Sauce (page 40), a bright purée of wild huckleberries, wild garlic, and olive oil, for an authentic taste of the Pacific Northwest, courtesy of a chef friend of the Skokomish tribe. Stash an extra pint of Khoresh Fesenjoon (page 82)— a Persian stew of pomegranate molasses, walnuts, and sweet spices—in your freezer to turn cubes of any protein into a remarkably tasty topping for couscous.

Through these recipes and stories, Mark teaches us the rewards that await when we step out of our comfort zones and into the unknown with a listening ear, an open heart, and a hungry belly.

Grab your saucepan, and let the tour begin.

SUSAN PUCKETT
Atlanta, Georgia

Author of *Eat Drink Delta: A Hungry Traveler's Journey through the Soul of the South* and coauthor of *Turnip Greens & Tortillas* with chef Eddie Hernandez

Introduction

A FEW YEARS AGO, I SET OUT INTO THE WORLD WITH two ultimately successful and intertwined missions. The first was writing a travel cookbook called *Cooking with Spices*. The second was completing the Continent Grand Slam: visiting all seven continents in one calendar year. In Antarctica, the landscape was breathtaking and otherworldly, even if our culinary panorama was limited to our vessel's galley, lest we end up like Ernest Shackleton and made to survive on penguin. Charles and Miranda Shackleton, relatives of the famous explorer, happened to be on the same expedition trip. Upon our return to the tip of South America, they invited me to their farm in Vermont to finish the final chapters of the book, and I duly obliged.

People invite me into their homes and feed me quite often. You might say it's luck, but it keeps occurring. It coincidentally is also my preference to be had over for dinner versus attending a stuffy, crowded tourist attraction. Besides, I usually find the layout of a local kitchen to be more culturally indicative than the region's highest art or classic architecture. It is in those cooking spaces that the secrets to what is really valued are revealed, usually to my pleasant surprise. Marveling at how pans are stored, or how the boxy cheese grater is identical to my Nonna's in Italy, are paramount cultural indicators from my perspective and how I get my kicks.

It is in this spirit that this book is written. I was told when I was quite young that you are who you surround yourself with. That seemed like an easy way to become a good, interesting person, as long as I was successful in finding good, interesting people and convincing them to let me stick around. Thankfully, you'll find such individuals between the covers of this book. Hopefully, people will keep opening their homes to me, feeding me, and teaching me the stories of their place, their family, and their kitchen. This book is a conduit to open those homes, and my own, to you—to share, as so many have done with me.

The Family of Sauces

Why sauces? As the saying goes, "What's sauce for the goose is sauce for the gander." While I wouldn't say sauces are a cultural universal, as are proverbs, they do have a widespread dispersion that's worthy of reverential contemplation. This book, in particular, takes you around the world of sauces with a traveler's mentality. On the road in a foreign land, seeing everything is impossible. If you try, you miss what is truly unique about a place. Books with 400-plus recipes claim to be exhaustive, yet many of them don't have Khoresh Fesenjoon (page 82) or Jajik (page 80). Are they truly acquainted with Persian cuisine? Have they been in the kitchen, or did they just go to the monuments?

Then there are the French mother sauces that require acknowledgment but have been comprehensively covered elsewhere. They form a necessary foundation to understand a certain side of how we use sauces in modern *Western* cuisine, and I've given you simple versions of a few of them starting on page xiii (along with recipes for stock and a basic mayonnaise). However, my hope is that you'll also devour keenly the recipes that are more difficult to pronounce. The rewards, I promise, will be boundless.

A recipe like Sambel Ulek (page 30) is a sugar-free candidate to replace your store-bought sriracha. Instead of run-of-the-mill plum sauce, make Tkemali (page 74) from Georgia, cooking it down to your desired thickness. When Georgian cuisine breaks into mainstream consciousness in the coming years (look it up; it's imminent), you'll be able to extoll the multipurpose virtues of blue fenugreek. This work curates a selection of sauces chosen primarily for versatility.

Distinguishing between a sauce and a dish can be tricky. My Nonna would not consider her ragù a sauce. Instead, ravioli con ragù is *a dish*. Nonetheless, her tomato sauce that serves as the source of Ragù della Nonna (page 108) is so versatile that I've made it with llama meat and gotten the nod of approval from my Italian mother.

CLASSIC SAUCES

Béchamel // MAKES ABOUT 2 CUPS

2½ cups whole milk

4 tablespoons unsalted butter or
   clarified butter

4 tablespoons all-purpose flour

Salt

Ground white pepper

Freshly grated nutmeg

1. In a medium saucepan over low heat, heat the milk until just before it scalds, about 2 to 5 minutes. Take it off the heat when you start to see little bubbles form around the edges. Set aside.

2. In a large, heavy-bottomed saucepan or skillet, heat the butter until the foam subsides (unless you're using clarified butter, then simply heat). Slowly add the flour, constantly whisking to form a smooth roux.

3. Add the heated milk to the skillet while whisking (to avoid clumping). Continue stirring until the sauce thickens and begins to lightly bubble.

4. Season with salt, pepper, and nutmeg, and remove from the heat.

Hollandaise // MAKES 1 CUP

1 stick (8 ounces) unsalted butter

Juice of ½ lemon

1 tablespoon apple cider vinegar

4 egg yolks, room temperature

1 tablespoon cold water

1. Clarify the butter by heating in a small skillet over low heat. Skim the white residue off as it arrives at a simmer until the butter is golden and clear, about 5 minutes. Set aside.

2. Bring a medium pot of water to a low simmer, and place a stainless steel bowl over it. Add the lemon juice and apple cider vinegar to the bowl, then add the egg yolks while whisking constantly.

3. Continuing to whisk, gradually add the warm butter until the mixture becomes thick. If the eggs begin to scramble, add cold water and mix. Strain out any thick lumps. Serve immediately.

Simple Tomato Sauce // MAKES ABOUT 2½ CUPS

½ cup extra-virgin olive oil

1 tablespoon tomato paste

1 (28-ounce can) San Marzano tomatoes

½ teaspoon crushed red pepper flakes (or up to 1 tablespoon to maximize heat)

½ cup roughly chopped fresh oregano leaves

Sea salt

Freshly ground black pepper

1. In a large saucepan over medium heat, heat the olive oil for 1 minute. Add the tomato paste, and let it heat for 1 to 2 minutes.

2. Add the tomatoes, stir, and cook. Sprinkle the red pepper and oregano on top.

3. Let simmer on medium-low heat for half an hour to 2 hours, until the sauce is thick and soupy. Season with salt and pepper.

4. Use right away, or let cool and freeze in smaller containers for later use.

Basic Mayonnaise // MAKES ABOUT 1 CUP

½ cup extra-virgin olive oil

½ cup avocado oil (or your oil of choice for flavor)

2 large egg yolks

2 teaspoons hot water

1 teaspoon white wine vinegar

1 teaspoon Dijon or yellow mustard

Salt

Ground white pepper

1 teaspoon freshly squeezed lemon juice (optional)

1. In a medium bowl, combine the oils.

2. In a separate medium bowl, whisk together the yolks, water, vinegar, and mustard until foamy. You can do this in a bowl by hand, or in a blender or food processor.

3. Add the oil gradually to the egg yolks, while hand-whisking or with the motor running. Begin with drops, whisking or blending simultaneously, and then add more drops as each is incorporated. Then advance to a thin stream, until all the oil is mixed in and the mayo is smooth.

4. Season with salt and pepper and, if using, lemon juice. Serve cold.

Stock // MAKES ABOUT 3 TO 4 CUPS

2 teaspoons vegetable oil

1 tablespoon chopped carrot

1 tablespoon chopped onion

1 tablespoon chopped celery

1 pound chicken bones, veal bones, nonstarchy vegetables, nonoily fish bones and/or heads or shellfish remains (shrimp, crawfish, crab, lobster)

1 quart cold water

1 fresh thyme sprig

1 dried bay leaf

1 small handful juniper berries

1 or 2 fresh sage leaves and stems

Salt

Freshly ground black pepper

1. In a large skillet over medium heat, heat the oil. Add the carrot, onion, and celery (known collectively as mirepoix), and cook for 1 minute.

2. Add bones or veggies, and cook until browned—the time will vary depending on what you're using.

3. Transfer everything to a stockpot, and add the water, thyme, bay leaf, juniper berries, and sage. Season with salt and pepper, and bring to a simmer over medium-high heat.

4. Simmer, covered, for the following lengths of time, skimming as necessary:

> → **VEGETABLES:** 30 minutes to 1 hour

> → **FISH AND SHELLFISH:** 45 minutes to 1 hour

> → **CHICKEN BONES:** 3 to 6 hours, adding liquid as necessary

> → **VEAL BONES:** 4 to 8 hours or all day

5. Strain through a fine mesh strainer and use, or let cool and freeze for later use.

How to Use This Book

This book is broken down into four world regions and features 15 sauces from each. The land masses each section covers are vast, but the recipes are specific. I've endeavored to dance between representation and familiarity. So instead of pico de gallo and salsa, I went to a native Chilean for Pebre (page 64), which combines elements of both.

Part One is structured by region, for you home cooks looking to get outside your comfort zone and push your boundaries. I've incorporated tips and suggestions to ensure you will not be overwhelmed on the journey. Once you understand the basics of each sauce, I'd suggest cooking the way I learned from my mother—by experimenting.

Each recipe comes with a useful chile icon, for both those who love heat and those who don't (for y'all, just cut back on or leave out the chiles). I'll include some flavor notes, as well, so if you're unfamiliar with the ingredients, you'll have some sense of where you'll end up. Under Pairings and Serving Ideas, I've suggested several mains and sides for each sauce.

Different regions define sauce differently. Some, like Thailand's Nam Jim (page 26), are used for dipping. Some are condiments, used to pour over a finished product, such as Tomatillo Salsa Verde (page 58). Others serve as a base for soups and stews, a marinade for proteins, or a classic sauce to cook in, like Coconut Curry (page 8). Where possible, I've indicated in the recipe how the sauce is typically used—or suggested various ways it can be used, such as pour over, cook in, condiment, marinade, and glaze, as is the case for Chef Seong's hypnotizing Gochujang "Seong" Sauce (page 20). This is what I mean by those labels:

→ **BASE:** use for more complex soups, sauces, and dishes

→ **CONDIMENT:** acts as an accompaniment, often cold, to a food to boost flavor

→ **COOK IN:** intended for a protein, grain, or base to be cooked in the sauce

→ **DIPPING:** a sauce put in a bowl or dish for a food to be dipped in

→ **GLAZE:** used to coat and/or baste a protein as it cooks

→ **MARINADE:** applied to a base ingredient before cooking to infuse flavor

→ **MIX IN:** combined with another sauce as a flavoring agent

→ **POUR OVER:** a sauce, often hot, that is simply poured over a main dish or side

→ **SPREAD:** a thicker sauce applied to bread or sandwiches

One of the main lessons I learned from speaking with readers about what they loved in *Cooking with Spices* was that sometimes you just have some "freakin' chicken" in the fridge and you don't know what to do with it. So in addition to the 60 sauce recipes, Part Two has more than 30 undemanding recipes for proteins, grains, vegetables, beans, and other legumes. You can mix and match a sauce and a base for a choose-your-own-journey approach to dinner.

Each recipe in Part Two has sauce pairing suggestions and recommendations on how and when to use them. The World Pantry (page 189) describes some of the less common ingredients you may not necessarily find on your local supermarket shelves. You'll see items like pomegranate molasses, palm sugar, fish sauce, and potato flour, for example.

It is my sincere hope that you haven't come across anything like this book, that you'll use it often, and that it inspires you to go further, to discover. Perhaps, after trying sauces from Zach Johnston and inspired by Brian Yazzie, that you'll lead your own investigation into indigenous chefs and foods. A good place to continue the journey is following Brian's work with The Sioux Chef, Sean Sherman.

Most of all, when you use the recipes in this book, may it remind you that through food, the good out there in the world is allowed to breathe. Perhaps it is during a big family meal that the political divide is melted, as happens with TJ's Toum (page 94). Or maybe you've been traveling in a foreign country and were helped without expectation, as I was in Spain when Manuel and his classmates rescued me from a depressive state and swept me to the houses of their parents in Portugal where I learned for the first time of Piri Piri Whiskey Sauce (page 118). People are still inviting strangers into their kitchens—the safe harbor to the rickety skiffs that are our traveling souls. The recipes in this book were given with love. And it is with love that I share them with you.

POMEGRANATE-BEET RAITA, PAGE 6

EXPLORING THE WORLD OF SAUCES

Cooks throughout the world use sauces to flavor and enrich their foods. This is an immense category that stretches to include curries, chutneys, marinades, gravies, condiments, and dipping sauces. In this part, I will introduce you to the world of flavors and ingredients that make up each of the cuisines spanned in these four chapters.

Sauces differ by region, but there are many threads that connect us. Zhoug (page 96) from Yemen and Chimichurri (page 66) from Argentina are cousins, separated—as many cousins are—only by spice content and cilantro preferences. Certain flavors might be familiar, but some will likely be distinctly foreign. However, I'd like to think that maybe it's akin to you having a flathead screwdriver (hot sauce), and here you'll find a Phillips-head (Sambel Ulek, page 30).

Each chapter acts as a culinary passport to explore a condensed area of a vast world region. Asia, the Indian Subcontinent, and Oceania, for example, is a considerable portion of the Earth. It was not easy to pick 15 distinct sauces that stretch from India and Pakistan to New Zealand. Rather than comprehensiveness, it is usefulness that resolves the balance. Part One is about being excited about learning world sauces and how to use them every day.

1

ASIA, INDIAN SUBCONTINENT, AND OCEANIA

NARROWING DOWN ASIA, OCEANIA, AND THE
Indian subcontinent into 15 diverse and useful sauce
recipes was perhaps my most arduous task in compiling
this book; such is the diversity and creativity of the
cuisines. To begin with, in many of the cultures
highlighted in this section, "sauce" has a loose definition. Sauces are
thought of for dipping or pouring or highlighting or using as a base. One
Sri Lankan mother communicated to me (through her daughter) that Sri
Lankans don't use sauces, while extolling the virtues of Mango Chutney
(page 12) and Coconut Curry (page 8).

Chiles (a spice that actually comes from the Americas) are the main
star of this region, with notable exceptions in the recipes from Japan and
New Zealand. My goal in this chapter is to give you a sauce that acts as
a "launching pad" into each cuisine and a different tool to put in your
culinary toolbox.

I've reached out to sources more authoritative than my own to present
sauces people are actually making out there in the world. But authority
is not always associated with authenticity. Conventional cookbook
wisdom would advise against including Tikka Masala (page 10), a dish
considered inauthentic but nevertheless eaten and enjoyed in Indian and
Bangladeshi restaurants within and outside of the Indian subcontinent.
Ingredients move and fuse, even if at times the circumstances driving
them are unpalatable. Tikka Masala in India has been imported to
accommodate Western palates. Still, the standards for this book are
deliciousness and versatility, and those benchmarks are what justify its
inclusion here.

Traditions evolve. New Zealand and Australia are perfect examples
of this: One must nod to the strong gastronomic cultures that existed
before European settlement nearly eviscerated them. Other countries
have sauces that seem to have been part of the culinary culture for as
long as there has been cuisine. I've long dreamed, while staring at the
Sambel Ulek jar in my fridge, of making it. My visit to Japan—really an
excuse to binge on ramen—was rich in sauces, including Ponzu (page 16)
and Tonkatsu (page 18). Perhaps Cambodian cuisine is not as well known
(in the West) as its neighbors, but if you've spent time in Cambodia,
you'll know that any fresh *amok* (made with Yellow Kroeung [page 24])
rivals any dish you've ever had.

Pomegranate-Beet Raita //

YOGURT SAUCE

GLUTEN FREE • NUT FREE • VEGETARIAN

PREP TIME:
15 MINUTES

COOK TIME:
10 MINUTES

MAKES:
ABOUT 1½ CUPS

FLAVOR NOTES
HONEYED
FRUITY
COOLING
AROMATIC

TYPE OF SAUCE
CONDIMENT
MIX IN
SPREAD
MARINADE

Raitas *are yogurt-based sauces geared toward offsetting the heat of masalas and curries (try it with Coconut Curry on page 8). It also works as a sauce or condiment for proteins. Hiding sweet treasures like pomegranate seeds, which are featured prominently in Pakistani and Indian cuisines, in with savory meats and veggies always achieves a tasteful surprise. It's hard not to love the alluring color and health component of beets as an addition to this cooling sauce.*

2 or 3 small beets, shredded

2 tablespoons extra-virgin
    olive oil, divided

1 shallot, chopped

1 garlic clove, chopped

½ teaspoon ground cumin

1 teaspoon black sesame seeds

1 cup full-fat yogurt

Squeeze of lemon juice

1 teaspoon salt

2 tablespoons
    pomegranate seeds

Several fresh mint leaves

SPECIAL EQUIPMENT NEEDED

Food processor

1. In a medium pan over medium heat, sauté the beets in 1 tablespoon of oil until soft, about 5 minutes. Add the shallots and garlic and cook for 1 to 2 minutes, or until golden brown (they'll turn red, too). Mix in the cumin. Let cool.

2. In a small skillet over medium-low heat, toast the sesame seeds for 1 to 2 minutes, until the aroma is revealed.

3. In a food processor, process the beets, shallots, and garlic with the remaining 1 tablespoon of olive oil.

4. In a medium bowl, fold the mixture into the yogurt. Add the sesame seeds, lemon juice, and salt.

5. Sprinkle the pomegranate seeds and mint on top.

STORAGE: *1 week in the refrigerator, in a glass jar or plastic container*

INGREDIENT TIP: *Use full-fat regular yogurt rather than Greek yogurt to make use of some of the liquid.*

REPURPOSING TIP: *Raita makes a great pre-workout snack, or use it as a marinade several hours ahead of cooking a protein.*

PAIRINGS AND
SERVING IDEAS

MAINS

Stovetop Lamb Loin
Chops (page 147)

Skirt Steak a la
Parrilla (page 144)

Grilled
Flanken-Style
Ribs (page 143)

Vegetable
Stir-Fry (page 169)

SIDES

Pan-Roasted
Veggies (page 171)

Mixed Green
Salad (page 170)

Quinoa and Lentils
(page 183)

Falafel

Naan and pita,
for dipping

Coconut Curry // EASY STARTER CURRY

DAIRY FREE • GLUTEN FREE • NUT FREE

PREP TIME:
20 MINUTES

COOK TIME:
1 HOUR
20 MINUTES

MAKES:
ABOUT 5 CUPS

FLAVOR NOTES

HEARTY
SWEET
SPICY
WARM

HEAT INDEX

TYPE OF SAUCE

COOK IN

Curries are vast and diverse, and at times incredibly regionally specific. Enter Cooking with Spices veteran Beeta Mohajeri, private chef to the stars and responsible for beetzeats.com. She had a tour with an Indian chef, who taught her the technique of getting the most flavor and fragrance out of curries. This recipe is hers. This is an ideal starter curry to familiarize any home chef. You can make it with the same amount of cubed chicken or beef, or go vegan with tofu or cauliflower. For anything except beef, the cook time in step 4 will be dramatically less. Check constantly or open up pieces to check.

1 tablespoon coconut oil

1½ pounds boneless diced lamb

2 teaspoons kosher salt

1 teaspoon freshly ground black pepper

1 yellow onion, finely diced

½ teaspoon crushed red pepper flakes

1 tablespoon grated fresh ginger

1 tablespoon minced garlic

2 tablespoons garam masala (see Ingredient tip)

1 teaspoon ground turmeric

3 cracked cardamom pods (or ½ teaspoon ground cardamom)

2 tablespoons tomato paste

1 (13.5-ounce) can full-fat coconut milk

¼ cup water

1½ cups cubed sweet potato

1 cup frozen peas

Fresh cilantro leaves, for garnish

Full-fat yogurt or freshly squeezed lemon juice (for Dairy Free), for garnish

SPECIAL EQUIPMENT NEEDED

Wok or large braising pan with a cover

1. In a wok over high heat, heat the coconut oil.

2. Season the lamb with salt and pepper. Add to the wok and cook, stirring, until slightly browned on all sides, 3 to 4 minutes. Add the onion and red pepper flakes. Cook for another minute, until the onion is slightly softened.

3. Add the ginger, garlic, garam masala, turmeric, and cardamom. Stir through the lamb, and cook for a few minutes more, until the spices have released their aromas. Add the tomato paste, and cook for another minute.

4. Add the coconut milk and water. Season with salt, stir, and bring to a boil. Turn down the heat to a simmer, cover, and cook for 30 minutes, stirring occasionally to prevent burning or sticking to the bottom.

5. Stir in the sweet potato and peas. Cook for another 30 to 40 minutes, until the lamb is tender and the vegetables are fully cooked. The curry will be nice and thick, and the sweet potato should break down a little to give it some body and sweetness.

6. Sprinkle fresh cilantro leaves on top. Drizzle with yogurt or lemon juice to brighten the flavor just before serving.

STORAGE: *1 week in the refrigerator, in a glass jar or plastic container*

INGREDIENT TIP: *Garam masala is a mixture of coriander, cumin, cardamom, black pepper, bay leaf, cinnamon, clove, mace, and nutmeg. You can start with using equal parts of each and then adjust to your preferences. It will always taste better if you grind and make your own spice mixes, rather than using the prepared ones.*

PAIRINGS AND
SERVING IDEAS

MAINS

Stovetop Lamb Loin Chops (page 147)

Sautéed Thin-Cut Pork Chops (page 146)

Pan-Seared Boneless Chicken Thighs (page 149)

Sautéed Shrimp (page 164)

Stovetop Mussels (page 162)

Firm tofu

SIDES

Roasted cauliflower

Basmati rice

Naan

Tikka Masala // MASALA SPICES WITH CREAM

GLUTEN FREE • NUT FREE

PREP TIME:
30 MINUTES

COOK TIME:
1 HOUR

MAKES:
1½ CUPS
(SAUCE ONLY)

FLAVOR NOTES

WARM
CREAMY
RESONANT
RICH

HEAT INDEX

TYPE OF SAUCE

COOK IN
POUR OVER

Origin accounts of Tikka Masala differ: a way to moisten dry murgh (chicken) tikka in Scotland's Indian restaurants, or the product of innovation by Bangladeshi chefs in London. Some Indian and Bangladeshi cookbooks do not include it, citing inauthenticity. They are correct in that regard. However, rightly or wrongly, people around the world eat this sauce. Shifting international foodways are avenues for adaptability, and there's no doubt that this is a popular, resourceful sauce. My take is a basic skeleton to get you started, allowing further improvisation. We use chicken here, but try it with your protein of choice, including lamb, white fish, or firm tofu for a vegetarian option.

3 tablespoons clarified butter or ghee, divided

2 shallots, chopped

2 garlic cloves, minced

1 (1-inch) piece fresh ginger, minced

1 tablespoon garam masala

1 teaspoon ground turmeric

⅓ cup heavy (whipping) cream

1 tablespoon tomato paste

1 cup Greek yogurt

2 teaspoons freshly squeezed lemon juice

1 teaspoon ground cayenne pepper

2 teaspoons sea salt

1¼ pounds boneless, skinless chicken thighs, cubed, or protein of choice

1. In a large, heavy skillet over medium heat, heat 2 tablespoons of clarified butter. Add the shallots and cook for 2 to 3 minutes, until they start to sweat. Add the garlic and ginger, and cook for a few minutes more, until all turn golden brown. Add the garam masala and turmeric, and stir for 1 minute to coat everything.

2. In a small bowl, mix the cream and tomato paste together. Add to the skillet, and bring to a simmer. After a minute, stir the mix once to bring it together. Add the yogurt and lemon juice. Add the cayenne pepper and salt, to taste, and adjust the seasonings to your heat preference.

3. In a separate medium skillet over medium-high heat, heat the remaining 1 tablespoon of clarified butter, add the chicken (or your protein of choice), stir to mix, and brown. Cover and cook for 5 to 10 minutes, until well heated.

4. Transfer the chicken to the skillet with the sauce and cook for 30 to 45 minutes, covered, until cooked through. You may need to cook it a little longer uncovered, until the chicken is done.

STORAGE: *2 to 3 weeks in the refrigerator, in a glass jar or plastic container, but best to use fresh*

REPURPOSING TIP: *Cream and tomato paste with masala spices is one of the most forgiving culinary painter's palettes. Add canned tomatoes, canned chipotle peppers in adobo, citrus zest (lemon, lime, or orange), or anything else you like to further enliven this sauce.*

PAIRINGS AND SERVING IDEAS

MAINS

Stovetop Lamb Loin Chops (page 147)

Pan-Seared Boneless Chicken Thighs (page 149)

Pan-Seared White Fish (page 161)

Sautéed Shrimp (page 164)

Stovetop Mussels (page 162)

Firm tofu

SIDES

Pan-Roasted Veggies (page 171)

Naan or pita, for dipping

Mango Chutney //

MANGO SWEET AND SOUR SAUCE

DAIRY FREE • GLUTEN FREE • NUT FREE • VEGAN

PREP TIME:
20 MINUTES,
PLUS 8 HOURS
TO MARINATE

COOK TIME:
25 MINUTES

MAKES:
ABOUT 2 CUPS

FLAVOR NOTES
TANGY
PIQUANT
VIVID
HONEYED

HEAT INDEX

TYPE OF SAUCE
DIPPING
CONDIMENT
MARINADE
MIX IN

"**Y**ou know who gets loved and remembered for bringing something to the party?" asks my Sri Lankan friend Sonali. "The person with the mango." There are many chutney variations out there, but mango is their overlord. I love fig season in Louisiana, so I was compelled to honor those purple emerald celeste figs growing in my backyard with this staple from the Indian subcontinent. You can substitute golden or red raisins for the figs in the off season, or use candied or dried figs. Put this chutney on anything you want to make delicious: chicken, duck, lamb, breads.... Use leftover chutney as a marinade for poultry or pork by covering the protein and letting it sit for several hours or overnight in the refrigerator.

1 pound ripe mangos, peeled
  and cubed

1 to 3 chipotle chiles in
  adobo, diced

½ cup brown sugar

1 (1-inch) piece fresh
  ginger, chopped

1 garlic clove, minced

2 kaffir lime leaves, deveined
  (see Ingredient tip)

¼ cup figs (optional)

1 tablespoon coconut oil

1 cup apple cider
  vinegar, divided

Salt

Freshly ground black pepper

1 tablespoon garam masala

1. In a large, non-reactive container, combine the mangos, chiles, sugar, ginger, garlic, lime leaves, and figs (if using), and let sit for several hours or overnight, covered, in the refrigerator.

2. In a medium saucepan over low heat, melt the coconut oil. Transfer the mango mixture to the pan. When warm, add ¾ cup of vinegar and bring to a simmer. Simmer for 15 minutes, stirring occasionally, until the sugar dissolves and the mangoes become soft.

3. Turn the heat to low, season with salt and pepper, add the garam masala and the remaining ¼ cup of vinegar, and simmer for 5 to 10 minutes more, until the mixture thickens and the liquid has cooked away.

4. Let cool before storing.

STORAGE: *2 weeks in the refrigerator, in a glass jar or plastic container*

INGREDIENT TIP: *Kaffir lime leaves will be the most difficult ingredient to track down, but some specialty stores have them. They're often dried, so they also ship well. I get mine from Red Stick Spice Company (see Resources on page 200).*

PAIRINGS AND
SERVING IDEAS

MAINS

Skirt Steak a la
Parrilla (page 144)

Grilled
Flanken-Style
Ribs (page 143)

Sautéed
Thin-Cut Pork
Chops (page 146)

Stovetop Lamb Loin
Chops (page 147)

Pan-Seared
Crispy-Skin Duck
Breast (page 150)

Pan-Seared
Boneless Chicken
Thighs (page 149)

Black Beans and
Wild Rice (page 186)

SIDES

Pan-Roasted
Veggies (page 171)

Duck Fat Fries
(page 176)

Roasted Fingerling
Potatoes (page 177)

Toast with cheese

Naan

Black Bean Sauce // STIR-FRY SAUCE

DAIRY FREE

PREP TIME:
20 MINUTES,
PLUS 30 MINUTES
TO SOAK

COOK TIME:
20 MINUTES

MAKES:
ABOUT ¾ TO 1 CUP

FLAVOR NOTES

EARTHY
TANGY
RESONANT
WARM

HEAT INDEX

TYPE OF SAUCE

COOK IN
MARINADE
CONDIMENT

Black Bean Sauce is a flavor you're no doubt familiar with if ever you've dined in a Chinese restaurant or dabbled in East Asian-inspired cuisine. It's made from fermented soybeans—unlike the black beans used in Latin cuisine—which are known as douchi. This sauce is incredibly easy to make at home and store for future use. Stir-fry is simply incomplete without it. Or put a smear in or on an omelet, or sauté tofu in Black Bean Sauce and garlic.

4 tablespoons fermented black beans (see Ingredient tip)

¼ cup peanut oil

1 (1-inch) piece fresh ginger, chopped

1 tablespoon soy sauce

2 teaspoons crushed red pepper flakes or 1 tablespoon chili paste, such as Sambel Ulek (page 30)

1 whole star anise pod

1 tablespoon oyster sauce (or Bragg Liquid Aminos)

2 scallions, green parts only, chopped

¼ cup mirin or rice wine

¼ cup chicken or vegetable stock (page xv)

½ teaspoon cornstarch dissolved in 1 teaspoon water

1 tablespoon freshly squeezed lemon juice

Salt

Freshly ground black pepper

1. Cover the black beans in cool or room temperature water for 30 minutes to allow them to reconstitute. Drain and rinse several times, pat dry, then chop or mash them.

2. In a medium saucepan over high heat, heat the oil until it lightly smokes, add the black beans and ginger, and cook, stirring, for 1 to 2 minutes.

3. Add the soy sauce, red pepper flakes, star anise, oyster sauce, and scallions, stirring constantly, and cook just until fragrant. Add the mirin and stock, and mix. Turn the heat to medium-low and let simmer for 10 minutes.

4. Add the cornstarch to thicken the sauce and the lemon juice to flavor. Season with salt and pepper.

STORAGE: *2 weeks in the refrigerator, in a glass jar or plastic container, or freeze in ice cube trays and transfer to a freezer bag for 3 to 6 months*

INGREDIENT TIP: *Fermented black beans can be found at most Asian markets and are easily ordered online.*

REPURPOSING TIP: *Shellfish are great cooked right as you make the black bean sauce. Simply switch to a wok or braising pan and add 2 to 3 pounds of mussels, clams, or shrimp (even snails) right before you add the mirin and stock in step 3.*

PAIRINGS AND
SERVING IDEAS

MAINS

Stovetop Lamb Loin
Chops (page 147)

Skirt Steak a la
Parrilla (page 144)

Pan-Seared
Boneless Chicken
Thighs (page 149)

Sautéed Shrimp
(page 164)

Stovetop Mussels
(page 162)

Vegetable
Stir-Fry (page 169)

SIDES

Hand-Cut Zucchini
Noodles (page 174)

Homemade Pasta
Noodles (page 184)

Oysters

Ponzu // CITRUS VINAIGRETTE

DAIRY FREE • NUT FREE

PREP TIME:
20 MINUTES,
PLUS AT LEAST A
DAY TO MARINATE

MAKES:
ABOUT 1½ CUPS

FLAVOR NOTES
SOUR
ASTRINGENT
CITRUSY
TANGY

TYPE OF SAUCE
POUR OVER
CONDIMENT
DIPPING
MIX IN

Ponzu is a Japanese staple sometimes described as akin to vinaigrette, but I've found its uses to be much broader. It really is a culinary workhorse, with a range from seafood to poultry, but can also be added to barbecue sauces, marinades, stir-fries, and dressings. Specific ponzu recipes are also closely guarded, so I was grateful when my friends Zanzuki and Satomi—whom I met while traveling in Japan—lent me theirs.

4 to 5 yellow yuzu, halved (or a mix of the juice of lemons and limes [4 to 5 total])

¾ cup dark soy sauce

1 teaspoon mirin or rice wine (optional)

5 grams dried kelp (kombu)

5 grams bonito flakes

SPECIAL EQUIPMENT NEEDED

Fine metal strainer

1. Cut the yuzu in half and juice them, being careful not to get any seeds. After squeezing once, press the pulp inside using a spoon to squeeze out the remaining juice.

2. In a glass container such as a clean bottle, mix the dark soy sauce and yuzu juice. Add the mirin (optional) to mellow out the flavor. Add the kelp and bonito flakes, mix, and refrigerate the container.

3. Marinate for at least 1 to 2 days, or up to 2 weeks. The longer it sits, the more delicious it becomes, and the sour taste will increase as well.

4. Use the strainer to strain out the kelp and bonito flakes. Transfer the sauce to another clean jar to store.

STORAGE: *6 months in the refrigerator, in a glass jar*

INGREDIENT TIP: *The base of this sauce is* dashi, *which is a stock made from dried kelp and bonito flakes. Mirin is a sweet Japanese rice cooking wine. You'll find them all at Japanese supermarkets or online.*

REPURPOSING TIP: *Ponzu can be thinned with oil and vinegar as a dressing or thickened by cooking down (add a bit of cornstarch to enhance the process).*

PAIRINGS AND SERVING IDEAS

MAINS

Skirt Steak a la Parrilla (page 144)

Pan-Seared Crispy-Skin Duck Breast (page 150)

Pan-Seared Boneless Chicken Thighs (page 149)

White Fish Four Ways (page 158)

Pan-Seared Sea Scallops (page 165)

SIDES

Quinoa and Lentils (page 183)

Shredded cabbage coleslaw

Tofu salad (*Hiyayakko* in Japanese)

Tonkatsu // TERIYAKI-STYLE BARBECUE SAUCE

DAIRY FREE • NUT FREE

PREP TIME:
5 MINUTES,
PLUS 1 TO 2 HOURS
TO MARINATE

COOK TIME:
10 MINUTES

MAKES:
ABOUT ½ CUP

FLAVOR NOTES

TANGY

SALTY

SWEET

SHARP

HEAT INDEX

TYPE OF SAUCE

POUR OVER

DIPPING

MARINADE

CONDIMENT

Tonkatsu is a complex and delicious Japanese barbecue sauce that can be used for all types of katsu-*style cooking (pork or other protein, coated and fried in panko breadcrumbs). It's a Western-style sauce—developed after the turn of the twentieth century. There are three types of this style of sauce (pronounced* so-su *in Japanese):* usutah *is thin like Worcestershire sauce;* chuno *is medium thick; and Tonkatsu is the thickest.*

1 teaspoon sesame seeds

3 tablespoons Worcestershire sauce (or Bragg Liquid Aminos)

2 tablespoons tomato paste

1 tablespoon brown sugar

1 tablespoon Dijon mustard

2 tablespoons mirin or rice wine

1 tablespoon soy sauce

¼ teaspoon crushed red pepper flakes

1 tablespoon oyster or fish sauce (see Ingredient tip)

1 tablespoon honey

1 teaspoon cornstarch dissolved in 2 teaspoons water

SPECIAL EQUIPMENT NEEDED

Mortar and pestle

1. In a small, dry skillet over medium-high heat, toast the sesame seeds for 1 to 2 minutes, until aromatic. Let cool, and crush in a mortar and pestle.

2. In a medium bowl, mix together the crushed seeds, Worcestershire, tomato paste, sugar, mustard, mirin, soy sauce, red pepper flakes, oyster sauce, and honey. Let sit for 1 to 2 hours.

3. Transfer the mixture to a small saucepan, set over medium heat, and cook just until the sugar is dissolved and the honey evenly spreads.

4. Add the cornstarch as it starts to simmer, and cook, stirring, for 1 or 2 minutes, until the sauce thickens.

STORAGE: *4 to 5 days in a glass jar*

INGREDIENT TIP: *Oyster sauce is widely available in supermarkets. You'll find fish sauce at most grocery stores in the international food aisle. For a vegan sauce, use Bragg Liquid Aminos instead of the oyster or fish sauce and Worcestershire.*

REPURPOSING TIP: *Pair Tonkatsu with Japanese mayonnaise—easily purchased at an international market—and wasabi. Mix 1 tablespoon wasabi powder with 1 tablespoon water and let sit for 10 minutes. Then add 4 tablespoons Japanese mayo, 1 teaspoon lemon zest, a dash of soy sauce, and 1 teaspoon Shichimi Togarashi (a spice blend that's equal parts sansho peppercorns, crushed red pepper flakes, dried orange peel, sesame seeds, ground ginger, shredded nori seaweed, and poppy seeds), or any spice blend you prefer.*

PAIRINGS AND
SERVING IDEAS

MAINS

Sautéed
Thin-Cut Pork
Chops (page 146)

Stovetop Lamb Loin
Chops (page 147)

Skirt Steak a la
Parrilla (page 144)

Pan-Seared
Crispy-Skin Duck
Breast (page 150)

Pan-Seared
Boneless Chicken
Thighs (page 149)

Turkey Breast
Scaloppini Style
(page 148)

Fried chicken

SIDES

Pan-Roasted
Veggies (page 171)

Duck Fat Fries
(page 176)

Tempura

Shredded cabbage
coleslaw

Gochujang "Seong" Sauce //

CHILI-GARLIC SAUCE

DAIRY FREE • NUT FREE • VEGETARIAN

PREP TIME:
5 MINUTES,
PLUS 1 HOUR TO
MARINATE

COOK TIME:
2 MINUTES

MAKES:
ABOUT 1 CUP

FLAVOR NOTES
SPICY
HOT
SWEET
SMOKY

HEAT INDEX

TYPE OF SAUCE
MARINADE
CONDIMENT
COOK IN
POUR OVER
GLAZE
BASE

Gochujang, *the base for this sauce, is a Korean chili paste made with chile peppers, rice powder, and a soybean paste called* doenjang. *It ferments in clay pots for months until it becomes rich and paste-like. Chef Seong Hwang, private chef to future NBA Hall of Famers, told me that as kids, he and his brother used to mix it with ketchup and mayo to use as a dip with snacks. You can also use it as a base for other dynamic sauces and marinades. A dish called* 불닭 *(bul-dak)—translated as "fire chicken"—is a typical dish that uses gochujang, but I eat it with a spoon as well.*

6 whole garlic cloves, peeled

¼ cup gochujang (Korean chili paste; see Ingredient tip)

¼ cup honey

2 tablespoons soy sauce

2 tablespoons rice vinegar

1 (1-inch piece) fresh ginger, grated

1 tablespoon toasted sesame oil

1. In a small skillet over medium heat, roast the peeled garlic cloves for 1 to 2 minutes, until fragrant, then mince.

2. In a small mixing bowl, combine the garlic, gochujang, honey, soy sauce, vinegar, ginger, and sesame oil.

3. Let sit at room temperature for an hour before transferring to a jar.

STORAGE: *1 month in the refrigerator, in a glass jar*

INGREDIENT TIP: *You can find gochujang in many stores, including Whole Foods. Annie Chun's is a well-known brand.*

REPURPOSING TIP: *You can adjust the thickness using more or less of the vinegar and sesame oil and tinker with the sweetness by adding a little corn syrup. Combine this sauce with mayonnaise for a spread or dipping sauce for seafood, sushi, or shellfish.*

PAIRINGS AND SERVING IDEAS

MAINS

Grilled Flanken-Style Ribs (page 143)

Sautéed Thin-Cut Pork Chops (page 146)

Stovetop Lamb Loin Chops (page 147)

Skirt Steak a la Parrilla (page 144)

Turkey Breast Scaloppini Style (page 148)

Pan-Seared Boneless Chicken Thighs (page 149)

Stovetop Mussels (page 162)

SIDES

Pan-Roasted Veggies (page 171)

Roasted Brussels sprouts

Grilled eggplant

Steamed asparagus

Nuoc Mam Cham // DIPPING FISH SAUCE

DAIRY FREE · GLUTEN FREE · NUT FREE

PREP TIME:
5 MINUTES

MAKES:
ABOUT ½ CUP

FLAVOR NOTES
SWEET
SOUR
SPICY
SAVORY

HEAT INDEX

TYPE OF SAUCE
DIPPING

Nuoc mam *is the quintessential sauce of Vietnam, according to Chef Nini Nguyen, who graces Season 16 of* Top Chef. *Her inside joke is that nuoc mam is to Vietnam as ketchup is to Americans: It goes on everything. There are regional differences. "In the north, they use vinegar for the acid, and in the south, they use coconut water for sweetness," said Chef Nini. She also said you can substitute ginger for the garlic, especially when using this sauce with fish.*

2 whole garlic cloves

1 to 3 bird's eye chiles, fresh or frozen

¼ cup sugar

¼ cup fish sauce

¼ cup freshly squeezed lime juice

SPECIAL EQUIPMENT NEEDED

Mortar and pestle (or chef's knife)

1. In the mortar and pestle, crush the garlic and chiles until they form a paste. Or crush the ingredients with the side of a chef's knife. You can add some of the sugar to help you achieve the paste consistency.

2. Transfer to a small bowl. Add the rest of the sugar, and mix very well.

3. Add the fish sauce and lime juice, and stir until the sugar is dissolved.

STORAGE: *1 to 2 weeks, in a glass jar or plastic container*

REPURPOSING TIP: *You can use this sauce as brine for pickling. Chef Nini recommends using julienned carrots. Leave them in for at least a day before eating.*

PAIRINGS AND
SERVING IDEAS

MAINS

Pan-Seared
Boneless Chicken
Thighs (page 149)

Pan-Seared Salmon
(page 157)

Grilled Salmon
(page 156)

Pan-Seared White
Fish (page 161)

Grilled White
Fish (page 159)

Pan-Seared Sea
Scallops (page 165)

Stovetop Mussels
(page 162)

Sautéed Shrimp
(page 164)

Vegetable
Stir-Fry (page 169)

SIDES

Homemade Pasta
Noodles (page 184)

Hand-Cut Zucchini
Noodles (page 174)

Pan-Roasted
Veggies (page 171)

Eggrolls

Lettuce wraps

Yellow Kroeung // LEMONGRASS CURRY

DAIRY FREE • GLUTEN FREE • NUT FREE

PREP TIME:
20 MINUTES,
PLUS 20 MINUTES
TO SOAK

COOK TIME:
15 MINUTES

MAKES:
ABOUT 3 CUPS

FLAVOR NOTES

WARM
SHARP
SPICY
CREAMY

HEAT INDEX

TYPE OF SAUCE

COOK IN
MARINADE
POUR OVER
DIPPING

I was immediately smitten during my time in Cambodia with fish amok, a popular Khmer dish featuring kaffir lime leaves and lemongrass that uses kroeung paste as a base. Kroeung paste is a Cambodian staple. It comes in three colors—yellow, green, and red. The yellow comes from turmeric, the green from lemongrass and cilantro, and the red from chiles. I asked my friend Lin, who is from Siem Reap, for advice on this recipe. She mentioned that condensed milk is often favored to palm sugar as a variation on this delicious curry.

2 dried chiles

2 fresh lemongrass stalks (cores only), sliced into rounds

1 teaspoon fish sauce

6 garlic cloves, crushed

10 kaffir lime leaves, deveined (see Ingredient tip)

2 tablespoons vegetable oil, divided

2 shallots, diced

1 (13.5-ounce) can full-fat coconut milk

2 whole star anise pods

1 teaspoon ground turmeric or 1-inch piece fresh, minced

1 teaspoon dried galangal or 1-inch piece fresh, minced (see Ingredient tip)

1 teaspoon granulated palm sugar or sweetened condensed milk

Salt

SPECIAL EQUIPMENT NEEDED

Food processor

1. Let the chiles soak in a small bowl of warm water for 20 minutes to reconstitute while you prepare the other ingredients. Drain well, then remove the seeds and stems.

2. In the food processor, grind together the lemongrass, fish sauce, garlic, lime leaves, chiles, and 1 tablespoon of oil to make the kroeung paste.

3. In a medium saucepan over low heat, heat the remaining 1 tablespoon of oil. Add the shallots and cook until slightly translucent, 2 minutes or so. Add the kroeung paste and simmer for 2 to 3 minutes, until it slightly browns.

4. Add the coconut milk, star anise, turmeric, galangal, and sugar, and stir. Let simmer for 10 minutes, or until the coconut milk is smooth. Season with salt.

STORAGE: *4 to 5 days in the refrigerator, in a glass jar or plastic container*

INGREDIENT TIP: *Galangal is a cousin of ginger and can be ordered dried on the Internet. Though not ideal, you can substitute lime zest and a squeeze of lemon juice for kaffir lime leaves.*

REPURPOSING TIP: *There is a lot of room to play with taste and color. Add more basic chili paste and leave out the turmeric for more of a red kroeung. Cook your protein of choice in the sauce by adding it at the end of step 3, and simmer until cooked through.*

PAIRINGS AND SERVING IDEAS

MAINS

Pan-Seared
Boneless Chicken
Thighs (page 149)

White Fish in
Parchment
(page 158)

Sautéed Shrimp
(page 164)

Stovetop Mussels
(page 162)

Vegetable
Stir-Fry (page 169)

Ground beef

SIDES

Pan-Roasted
Veggies (page 171)

Tofu

Rice

Nam Jim // SWEET AND SOUR SAUCE

DAIRY FREE • GLUTEN FREE • NUT FREE

PREP TIME:
30 MINUTES,
PLUS 30 MINUTES
TO STEEP

COOK TIME:
15 MINUTES

MAKES:
ABOUT ¾ CUP

FLAVOR NOTES

FRAGRANT
SWEET
SPICY
VIVID

HEAT INDEX

TYPE OF SAUCE

DIPPING
CONDIMENT
BASE

Thai cuisine is full of rich sauces and condiments. Nam Jim *means "dipping sauce" in Thai, and there are many kinds. This sauce is a sweeter chili sauce that is commonplace on Thai and Laotian tables. It also serves as the base for other Thai dipping sauces, made by adding more ingredients. Alyssa Han, owner of* Food and Arts by Alyssa*—an eco-friendly Thai cooking retreat outside Bangkok—graciously provided this recipe that works with Thai appetizers as well as steamed and grilled meats. To make the sauce vegan, use soy sauce or Bragg Liquid Aminos instead of fish sauce.*

FOR THE TAMARIND SAUCE

1¼ cups water

7 tablespoons seedless
tamarind pulp

¼ cup fish sauce

¼ cup granulated palm sugar

2 tablespoons white vinegar

2 tablespoons superfine or
caster sugar

FOR NAM JIM

2 tablespoons dried serrano
chiles (or chiles of choice)
soaked in warm water for
30 minutes and drained

1 tablespoon minced garlic

1 tablespoon chopped shallot

1 tablespoon chopped
coriander root (or chopped

fresh cilantro stalk and
1 teaspoon ground cumin;
see Ingredient tip)

1 tablespoon chopped onion

1½ tablespoons vegetable oil

Salt

SPECIAL EQUIPMENT NEEDED

Blender or food processor

TO MAKE THE TAMARIND SAUCE

1. In a small saucepan, boil the water. Take the pan off the heat, and add the tamarind pulp. Remove from the heat, let sit for 30 minutes, and stir until mixed. Squeeze through a sieve to remove any pulp or plant mass. You should end up with just over ¾ cups liquid concentrate. Add a bit more water if necessary.

2. Heat a wok or large skillet over high heat. Add your tamarind concentrate, and bring to a boil. Add the fish sauce and then the palm sugar.

3. When everything is dissolved, add the vinegar and caster sugar. Turn the heat to low and cook for 5 minutes, until the tamarind sauce is thick and syrupy. Set aside.

TO MAKE THE NAM JIM

1. In the food processor, blend the chiles, garlic, shallot, coriander root, onion, and 3 tablespoons of your tamarind sauce until you have a paste.

2. In a small skillet over medium heat, heat the oil. Add the paste, and bring to a simmering boil. Stir to combine.

3. Lower the heat. Add the remainder of the tamarind sauce, and season with salt. Remove from the heat and let cool.

STORAGE: *2 to 3 weeks in the refrigerator, in a glass jar or plastic container*

INGREDIENT TIP: *Asian or Indian specialty markets will likely have cilantro with the roots still attached. Another trick is to ask a neighborhood Thai restaurant if you can buy some of theirs during their next order.*

PAIRINGS AND SERVING IDEAS

MAINS

Pan-Seared Crispy-Skin Duck Breast (page 150)

Pan-Seared Boneless Chicken Thighs (page 149)

Vegetable Stir-Fry (page 169)

SIDES

Pan-Roasted Veggies (page 171)

Mixed Green Salad (page 170)

Oysters

Satay // PEANUT SAUCE

DAIRY FREE • GLUTEN FREE

PREP TIME:
10 MINUTES

COOK TIME:
20 MINUTES

MAKES:
ABOUT 1 CUP

FLAVOR NOTES

SWEET

SPICY

SALTY

NUTTY

HEAT INDEX

TYPE OF SAUCE

DIPPING

CONDIMENT

COOK IN

MARINADE

POUR OVER

The satay expertise here belongs to Tanny Jiraprapasuke, whose mother, Kanya, owned and operated a Thai restaurant in the 1980s when Thai food was starting to emerge in their adopted home of Glendale, California. Tanny told me many dishes had to be altered for the American palate, but satay (and pad Thai) were not among them. She said, "Even though satay is street food in Thailand, we always felt that there is something celebratory about the sauce. We only had it when there was a birthday or a big party."

1¼ cups water

7 tablespoons seedless tamarind pulp

½ cup raw peanuts

1 tablespoon extra-virgin olive oil or peanut oil

1 to 2 tablespoons Thai red curry paste (see Ingredient tip)

4 tablespoons massaman curry paste (see Ingredient tip)

4.5 ounces full-fat coconut milk

1 to 2 tablespoons liquid coconut sugar

Pinch salt

½ teaspoon fish sauce

SPECIAL EQUIPMENT NEEDED

Mortar and pestle

1. In a small saucepan, boil the water. Take the pan off the heat, and add the tamarind pulp, stir until mixed, remove from the heat, and let sit for 30 minutes. Squeeze through a sieve to remove any pulp or plant mass. Save what you don't use for future use (like in Nam Jim, page 26).

2. In a dry, medium pan over low heat, roast the peanuts until slightly charred (not burned), about 10 minutes. Place in the mortar with the oil, and work the peanuts into a chunky paste. This takes a little while but is worth the effort.

3. In a nonstick medium pot over medium heat, slightly sauté the red curry and massaman curry pastes, continuously stirring with a wooden spoon, for about 1 minute.

4. Slowly add some of the coconut milk into the pot, and continue to stir until the liquid evaporates. Then add a little more coconut milk and continue to stir the mixture for 3 to 4 minutes more.

5. Add the rest of the coconut milk and the peanut paste, coconut sugar, and 2 to 3 tablespoons of the liquid tamarind pulp. Continue to stir and allow the sauce to bubble and thicken. Add a pinch of salt, stir, then add the fish sauce to taste. Let cool.

STORAGE: *1 week in the refrigerator, in a glass jar*

INGREDIENT TIP: *You can find both massaman and red curry paste in Asian grocery stores or online in small jars or cans.*

REPURPOSING TIP: *The char on the peanuts adds a smokier flavor. You can freshen up leftover sauce by adding some coconut milk or even half and half and heating it on low on the stovetop. Then, right before serving, add ½ teaspoon of red chili oil. This will brighten the color and add a silkier texture.*

PAIRINGS AND
SERVING IDEAS

MAINS

Sautéed
Thin-Cut Pork
Chops (page 146)

Stovetop Lamb Loin
Chops (page 147)

Pan-Seared
Boneless Chicken
Thighs (page 149)

Pan-Seared
Crispy-Skin Duck
Breast (page 150)

Pan-Seared Sea
Scallops (page 165)

Stovetop Mussels
(page 162)

Sautéed Shrimp
(page 164)

Vegetable
Stir-Fry (page 169)

SIDES

Duck Fat Fries
(page 176)

Cold noodle salad

Sambel Ulek // CHILI SAUCE

DAIRY FREE • GLUTEN FREE • NUT FREE • VEGAN

PREP TIME:
30 MINUTES

COOK TIME:
10 MINUTES

MAKES:
ABOUT 1⅓ CUPS

FLAVOR NOTES
SPICY
PUNGENT
SHARP
BITING

HEAT INDEX

TYPE OF SAUCE
CONDIMENT
BASE
DIPPING
COOK IN

Sambel Ulek *is an extremely popular Indonesian chili sauce traditionally ground using a special mortar and pestle called a* cobek *and* ulekan—*hence the name. Perhaps you've seen the bottle at the store in the hot sauce aisle, labeled Sambal Oelek (a timeworn way the Dutch spelled it, apparently). One of the reasons to make your own Sambel Ulek (besides homemade always beating store bought) rather than using, say, sriracha, is there's very little sugar. Plus you can then cook sambel goring,* chili stir-fry. *Jeanie Laksmi of Bandung on West Java imparted her wisdom for this recipe.*

15 or 16 mini sweet red peppers or fresh big red chiles (such as merah besar, cayenne, serrano, or fireflame), seeded and stemmed (see Repurposing tip)

40 to 45 fresh green or red rawit or bird's eye chiles, seeded and stemmed (see Repurposing tip)

1 large or 2 small shallots, diced

1 tablespoon terasi shrimp paste (optional, omit for Vegan; see Ingredient tip)

1 tablespoon tomato paste

2 teaspoons salt

1 tablespoon coconut oil

1 teaspoon granulated palm sugar

SPECIAL EQUIPMENT NEEDED

Mortar and pestle or food processor

1. In a large pan over medium heat, fry the chiles, shallots, shrimp paste (if using), tomato paste, salt, coconut oil, and palm sugar until the chiles are cooked through, about 10 minutes. Open a window if using terasi shrimp paste, because it will stink to high heaven at first.

2. Let cool, then grind or process into a paste.

STORAGE: *3 to 4 weeks in the refrigerator, in a glass jar or plastic container*

INGREDIENT TIP: *Terasi shrimp makes this more authentically Indonesian. It is not the same thing as shrimp paste in bean oil, commonly found in the international aisle in the supermarket. Order online if you can't find it at an international market.*

REPURPOSING TIP: *Fresh green and sweet red peppers are mild alternatives to ease the heat for non-chileheads. To further decrease the heat, use green bird's eye chiles instead of red. To increase the heat, leave the seeds in. The sauce will become less hot as it sits in the refrigerator.*

PAIRINGS AND
SERVING IDEAS

MAINS

Grilled
Flanken-Style
Ribs (page 143)

Sautéed
Thin-Cut Pork
Chops (page 146)

Stovetop Lamb Loin
Chops (page 147)

Skirt Steak a la
Parrilla (page 144)

Pan-Seared
Boneless Chicken
Thighs (page 149)

SIDES

Quinoa and Lentils
(page 183)

Black Beans and
Wild Rice (page 186)

Rice

Spread on bread

Adobo // COCONUT MILK SAUCE

DAIRY FREE • GLUTEN FREE

PREP TIME:
5 MINUTES

COOK TIME:
15 MINUTES

MAKES:
ABOUT 1½ CUPS

FLAVOR NOTES

TANGY

SPICY

UMAMI

FULL

HEAT INDEX

🌶🌶🌶🌶🌶

TYPE OF SAUCE

COOK IN

BASE

*A**dobo is a national dish in the Philippines, though it's exceptionally regionally specific. Kim Suarez, senior editor of this book, graciously allowed me to share her mother's hyper-regional Adobo recipe, with the caveat that I include bay leaf, Kim's addition. Her mom puts black pepper in hers as a connection to Bicol, which is where Kim's grandfather is from. Bicol is comprised of islands in and around the southern end of Luzon Island. The cooking tends to use peppers and more heat and spice. As a nod to Kim's aunt, who puts achiote oil in her chicken Adobo, I've incorporated it here for a burst of color.*

2 tablespoons vegetable oil

3 to 4 garlic cloves, minced

1 pound medium to large shrimp, heads removed, shelled and deveined, or your protein of choice

¼ cup white vinegar (optional)

¼ teaspoon freshly ground black pepper

1 dried bay leaf

1 (13.5-ounce) can full-fat coconut milk, or 1 cup fresh (may be reduced to desired consistency)

Fish sauce or salt, for seasoning

1 small jalapeño pepper, halved lengthwise, seeded, and sliced

1 tablespoon achiote oil (see Ingredient tip)

2 scallions, green parts only, chopped, for garnish

1. In a large pan over medium heat, heat the oil. Sauté the garlic until golden brown and aromatic, about 2 minutes.

2. Add the shrimp, followed by the vinegar (if using), without stirring. When the liquid stars to boil, sprinkle in the pepper and add the bay leaf.

3. Pour in the coconut milk. Cook for about 2 minutes, until it boils. Season with fish sauce.

4. Add the sliced jalapeño and achiote oil, and cook for another 3 to 4 minutes. Take care to not overcook the shrimp or they will become rubbery and tough. They should be light and flavorful.

5. Remove from the heat, and serve garnished with the scallions.

STORAGE: *2 weeks in the refrigerator, in a glass jar or plastic container*

INGREDIENT TIP: *Make achiote oil by frying 1 tablespoon annatto seeds in ½ cup peanut oil for about 3 or 4 minutes. Strain out the seeds. Annatto (also called achiote) can be found in most Latin markets or ordered online.*

PAIRINGS AND
SERVING IDEAS

MAINS

Sautéed
Thin-Cut Pork
Chops (page 146)

Pan-Seared
Boneless Chicken
Thighs (page 149)

Pan-Seared
Crispy-Skin Duck
Breast (page 150)

Sautéed Shrimp
(page 164)

White Fish Four
Ways (page 158)

SIDES

Steamed white rice

Sauvignon Blanc Cream Sauce //

SILKY WHITE WINE SAUCE

GLUTEN FREE • NUT FREE • VEGETARIAN

PREP TIME:
10 MINUTES

COOK TIME:
20 MINUTES

MAKES:
ABOUT 1 CUP

FLAVOR NOTES

CREAMY
WARM
AROMATIC
BUTTERY

TYPE OF SAUCE

POUR OVER
COOK IN

New Zealand has a mix of colonist (specifically British) cuisine, native ingredients long used by indigenous peoples such as the Māori, and imported flavors from neighboring Southeast Asian countries. A traditional Māori hungi—in which a plethora of food is cooked underground using hot stones—is perhaps the most iconic gastronomic offering of the island. Alternatively, a versatile sauce descended from the European heritage of New Zealand is this superb cream sauce developed by Jack Hatzfeld, who was inspired by a version of this sauce while on a photography journey around the stunning South Island.

7 teaspoons butter, divided

1 shallot, diced

1 stalk fresh lemongrass, cut in 1-inch slices (optional; see Ingredient tip)

2 garlic cloves, whole

1 teaspoon white pepper

1¼ cups New Zealand Sauvignon Blanc

1½ teaspoons chopped fresh tarragon

1 tablespoon freshly squeezed lemon juice

1 teaspoon lemon zest

¾ cup heavy (whipping) cream

Salt

1. In a medium saucepan over medium-low heat, heat 1 teaspoon of butter. Add the shallots and lemongrass (if using), and cook for 2 to 3 minutes.

2. Add the garlic, white pepper, wine, tarragon, and lemon juice and zest. Bring to a simmer over medium-high heat, and cook for 6 minutes.

3. Remove the strips of lemongrass and garlic cloves, and add the remaining 6 teaspoons of butter. Cook until it melts. Add the cream.

4. Turn the heat to low and let simmer for 10 minutes. Season with salt.

STORAGE: *1 week in the refrigerator, in a glass jar or plastic container*

INGREDIENT TIP: *To cut lemongrass, you must chop off the top and bottom and bisect the stalk to remove the tough outer layers, revealing the tender inside.*

PAIRINGS AND
SERVING IDEAS

MAINS

**Turkey Breast
Scaloppini Style
(page 148)**

**Pan-Seared
Boneless Chicken
Thighs (page 149)**

**Grilled White
Fish (page 159)**

**Sautéed Shrimp
(page 164)**

**Baked Salmon
(page 156)**

**Stovetop Mussels
(page 162)**

**Hand-Rolled
Gnocchi (page 187)**

**Homemade Pasta
Noodles (page 184)**

SIDES

**Pan-Roasted
Veggies (page 171)**

**Hand-Cut Zucchini
Noodles (page 174)**

2

AMERICAS

IF YOU HANG OUT LONG ENOUGH IN A BAR IN BUENOS
Aires—where the Chimichurri recipe in this chapter originates
(page 66)—you'll eventually hear an Argentine complain about
the proprietorship of the word "American" by citizens of the
United States. They're not wrong. As South Americans, they're
Americans, too.

Before the establishment of modern borders, the Americas were
just one connected land mass. And there was a time when this land was
likely more united under a spirit of collectivity than it is today. Look to
3,000-year-old stores of quinoa found in Ontario, Canada, as proof of the
previously undescribed trade networks—long known to Native peoples—
that existed in this part of the world.

It is in this character that the recipes in this chapter lead from one to
another. The food found here is cooked in homes every day and paired
with all manner of ingredients, which is what versatile cooking is all
about. After all, this region is responsible for pumpkins, tomatoes, corn,
potatoes, chile peppers, avocados, chocolate, and spices like annatto,
pepitas, vanilla, and allspice.

The Americas is where adaptable sauces blossom, though this is partly
due to the involuntary colonial influence on the region. We sometimes
hear words like "unsophisticated" to describe the cuisine of the Americas,
but this region has a diverse culinary backbone that is on full display in
its regional sauces.

Oftentimes, "American" foods are thought of as either Latin dishes or
watered-down derivations of European cuisine. However, long before the
Europeans came, the foodways of the Americas were whole and diverse.
Along with simplified versions of classics like Mexican Mole (page 56)
and Cuban Mojito (page 52), you'll also notice a disproportionate number
of sauces from the United States. I am proud to highlight indigenous
chefs and ingredients, beginning in this section with a sauce from
Zach Johnston featuring a purely American ingredient—huckleberry
(page 40)—and one inspired by discussions with Navajo chef Brian
Yazzie, featuring squash (page 50).

Huckleberry Sauce // FOREST BERRY SAUCE

DAIRY FREE • GLUTEN FREE • NUT FREE • VEGAN

PREP TIME:
5 MINUTES

MAKES:
ABOUT 1½ CUPS

FLAVOR NOTES

EARTHY
UMAMI
SHARP
SWEET

TYPE OF SAUCE

CONDIMENT
GLAZE
POUR OVER
COOK IN

"Huckleberries were the sweet cornerstone of Salish cooking for the indigenous communities of the Pacific Northwest," Zach Johnston, of the Skokomish tribe of Washington, told me while teaching me about this huckleberry sauce that he makes after foraging. Huckleberries' sweetness will vary depending on the time of year they are harvested. Early in the season, they are grassy and tart; later, they are sweet and earthy. Both flavor profiles work well on all types of wild fish, gamey or farmed meats, and steak.

1 cup fresh huckleberries, stemmed and thoroughly washed (see Ingredient tip)

½ cup chopped fresh ramps (wild garlic; see Ingredient tip)

½ cup extra-virgin olive oil

Salt

Freshly ground black pepper

SPECIAL EQUIPMENT NEEDED

Blender or food processor

1. In a food processor or blender, combine the berries, ramps, and oil and blend into a paste. Add salt a pinch at a time until you taste the full profile of the berries. Sprinkle on pepper to taste.

2. Use this sauce on filets of salmon, halibut, trout, steak, or duck by smothering the entire top side of the protein with a thick layer of sauce, until the flesh is no longer visible.

3. Place the protein on a wood slab on a high-heat fire or grill.

4. The sauce should bubble just as the protein reaches ideal internal temperature (130° to 150°F for fish). Add more sauce as a baste if the protein needs more time to cook.

STORAGE: *1 week in the refrigerator, in a glass jar*

INGREDIENT TIP: *Fresh huckleberries are very easily found online and are often shipped overnight. You can substitute blueberries, or any forest fruit, for the huckleberries, but know that cultivated berries are generally sweeter than necessary for this kind of sauce. So look for tart ones that don't over-sweeten the dish. Frozen ones are fine in this recipe; let them thaw to room temperature before using.*

INGREDIENT TIP: *If you can't find ramps, you can use the green part of spring onions, scallions, or a leek.*

PAIRINGS AND SERVING IDEAS

MAINS

Skirt Steak a la Parrilla (page 144)

Grilled Salmon (page 156)

Grilled White Fish (page 159)

Pan-Seared Sea Scallops (page 165)

Stovetop Mussels (page 162)

Sautéed Shrimp (page 164)

Homemade Pasta Noodles (page 184)

Bison burgers

———

SIDES

Smashed Garlic Red Potatoes (page 176)

Scalloped potatoes

Wild rice

"Catch-All" Barbecue Sauce //

EVERYDAY BARBECUE SAUCE

DAIRY FREE • GLUTEN FREE • NUT FREE • VEGAN

PREP TIME:
10 MINUTES

MAKES:
ABOUT 2½ CUPS

FLAVOR NOTES
SMOKY
TANGY
SWEET
SOUR

HEAT INDEX

TYPE OF SAUCE
COOK IN
POUR OVER
MARINADE

I asked my friend Matt Moore, author of The South's Best Butts, to contribute a good starter barbecue sauce. He told me that throughout North Carolina, "one would be taken out back if the likes of sugar and tomato made their way into any said sauce. But being the Georgia boy that I am, now by way of Tennessee, the barbecue trail becomes more and more muddled as you make your way westward. Though I'm a vinegar purist, I've found that a touch of tomato and sugar, along with a few other catch-all ingredients, can sure round up as many palates as possible—making believers out of most. This is my go-to sauce for pork, chicken, and sausages. Just keep it away from beef, as you should never put vinegar on smoked beef. Skipping the allspice is a sin; it's the spice that makes this sauce feel like a family secret."

2 cups good-quality, raw, unfiltered apple cider vinegar

2 tablespoons tomato paste

2 tablespoons brown sugar

1 tablespoon kosher salt

1 tablespoon freshly ground black pepper

1 teaspoon garlic powder

1 teaspoon ground cayenne pepper

½ teaspoon ground allspice

1. In a jar with a lid, combine the vinegar, tomato paste, sugar, salt, black pepper, garlic powder, cayenne pepper, and allspice. Seal and shake vigorously until everything is evenly distributed.

2. Use immediately, or refrigerate. Shake before using.

STORAGE: *1 month in the refrigerator in a glass jar, or freeze in an ice cube tray and keep 3 months in the freezer in a freezer bag*

REPURPOSING TIP: *Liven up slaws and potato salad with a dash of this sauce, or use it as a marinade or baste while cooking.*

PAIRINGS AND
SERVING IDEAS

MAINS

Sautéed
Thin-Cut Pork
Chops (page 146)

Stovetop Lamb Loin
Chops (page 147)

Pan-Seared
Boneless Chicken
Thighs (page 149)

Burgers and
sausages

Hot dogs

Pulled pork

SIDES

Pan-Roasted
Veggies (page 171)

Black Beans and
Wild Rice (page 186)

'Merican Cheese Sauce //

USE-FOR-EVERYTHING CHEESE SAUCE

NUT FREE • VEGETARIAN

PREP TIME:
10 MINUTES

COOK TIME:
10 MINUTES

MAKES:
ABOUT 2½ CUPS

FLAVOR NOTES
CREAMY
WARM
BUTTERY
FILLING

TYPE OF SAUCE
COOK IN
POUR OVER

This sauce is from a truly modern American source: fake foods that developed out of TV dinners and ready-made dishes of the 1980s. It's like an additive-free Velveeta that can go on true Midwestern, Americanized staples like nachos, macaroni, and burgers. It was graciously provided by food writer and world traveler Steve Bramucci, who says, "This sauce will make you weep. So American yet so refined."

4 tablespoons butter

1 tablespoon finely minced onion

1 tablespoon finely minced garlic

¼ cup all-purpose flour

1½ cups whole milk, at room temperature

1 cup cubed or grated aged Cheddar cheese

1 tablespoon freshly ground black pepper

Pinch MSG (see Ingredient tip)

Salt

1. In a medium saucepan over medium heat, melt the butter. Once the foam has dissipated, add the onion and garlic and sauté for 2 minutes, stirring constantly.

2. Add the flour, and turn the heat to medium-low. Keep stirring to make a quick roux.

3. Slowly add the milk, while stirring to avoid clumping. Incorporate the cheese, pepper, and MSG, and stir until the cheese is evenly melted, about 5 minutes. Season with salt.

4. Remove from the heat and use immediately.

STORAGE: *2 weeks in the refrigerator, in a glass jar or plastic container*

INGREDIENT TIP: *MSG has a bad reputation, but there is a lot of false propaganda out there. It's a naturally occurring salt from an amino acid, and is found naturally in tomatoes, grapes, cheese, mushrooms, and other foods. It can truly heighten the flavors of a dish.*

REPURPOSING TIP: *Add nutritional yeast or whey protein–based "cheese powder" for an umami kick. Add stewed tomatoes and chopped jalapeños for queso.*

PAIRINGS AND
SERVING IDEAS

MAINS

Burgers

Hot dogs

Nachos

SIDES

Pan-Roasted
Veggies (page 171)

Roasted Fingerling
Potatoes (page 177)

Homemade Pasta
Noodles (page 184)

Hand-Rolled
Gnocchi (page 187)

Creole Remoulade and Comeback Sauce // COUSIN SAUCES FROM THE SOUTH

NUT FREE • VEGETARIAN

PREP TIME:
5 MINUTES

MAKES:
ABOUT 1 CUP

FLAVOR NOTES
CREAMY
TANGY
FRESH
SPICY

HEAT INDEX
🌶🌶🌶🌶

TYPE OF SAUCE
CONDIMENT

Creole Remoulade is based on the French sauce remoulade, made with mayonnaise or aioli (mayo seasoned with garlic). The Louisiana variety, though, is reddish and spicy. As a resident of New Orleans, I enjoy this recipe from Louisiana native Chris LeBlanc and his family. We drive down to Plaquemines Parish in winter to pick the citrus. The grapefruits are colossal, and the ones in Buras, Louisiana, are like flavor bombs ready to explode. Comeback Sauce is the kissin' cousin to Creole Remoulade. Martha Hall Foose—2009 James Beard award winner for Best American Cookbook—calls it "heaven on a cracker." Folks keep coming back for it time and time again.

FOR THE REMOULADE

1 cup mayonnaise

1½ teaspoons freshly squeezed grapefruit juice

1½ teaspoons freshly squeezed lemon juice

2 tablespoons creole mustard or Dijon mustard

1 tablespoon chopped capers

Several dashes Worcestershire sauce or Bragg Liquid Aminos

1 tablespoon finely chopped flat-leaf parsley

1 scallion, finely chopped

1 tablespoon Tabasco sauce

2 garlic cloves, minced

1 teaspoon local honey (optional)

Ground cayenne pepper

Salt

FOR THE COMEBACK SAUCE

1 cup mayonnaise

½ onion, grated

2 tablespoons creole mustard
or Dijon mustard

Several dashes Worcestershire
sauce or Bragg
Liquid Aminos

1 scallion, finely chopped

1 tablespoon Tabasco sauce

1 tablespoon paprika

2 garlic cloves, minced

1 teaspoon local honey
(optional)

Ground cayenne pepper

Salt

TO MAKE THE REMOULADE

In a large bowl, mix together the mayonnaise, grapefruit juice,
lemon juice, mustard, capers, Worcestershire, parsley, scallion,
Tabasco, garlic, and honey. Season to taste with the cayenne and
salt, and keep refrigerated until ready to serve.

TO MAKE THE COMEBACK SAUCE

In a large bowl, mix together the mayonnaise, onion, mustard,
Worcestershire, scallion, Tabasco, paprika, garlic, and honey.
Season to taste with the cayenne and salt, and keep refrigerated
until ready to serve.

STORAGE: *2 weeks in the refrigerator, in a glass jar or plastic container*

REPURPOSING TIP: *Make your deviled eggs with this fiery remoulade.*

PAIRINGS AND
SERVING IDEAS

MAINS

Stovetop Lamb Loin
Chops (page 147)

Skirt Steak a la
Parrilla (page 144)

Grilled Salmon
(page 156)

Pan-Seared Sea
Scallops (page 165)

Stovetop Mussels
(page 162)

SIDES

Oven-Baked Potato
Chips (page 175)

Duck Fat Fries
(page 176)

Grilled vegetables

Steamed asparagus

Roasted Brussels
sprouts

Green Chile "Chacon" //

NEW MEXICAN CHILI SAUCE

DAIRY FREE • NUT FREE

PREP TIME:
10 MINUTES,
PLUS 30 MINUTES
TO COOL

COOK TIME:
2 HOURS
25 MINUTES

MAKES:
ABOUT 4 TO
5 CUPS

FLAVOR NOTES
SPICY
WARM
PIQUANT
BITING

HEAT INDEX

TYPE OF SAUCE
POUR OVER
COOK IN
MIX IN

Green chile dances on the taste buds of most visitors to the Land of Enchantment; such is the unbridled flavor of New Mexico's Hatch and Lemitar varieties of green chile peppers. They can be ordered online, but in a pinch, you can use a mix of Anaheim chiles and/ or (gulp!) jalapeños. Though this is a seasonal recipe—dependent on when you can get the capsicums—I consider a green chile-doused burrito at Albuquerque restaurant Frontier a strong candidate for my response when asked my choice for a last meal. So it's worth the wait. This is a dish in itself but can also be poured generously on tacos, arepas, or beans and rice. It comes from the Chacon family, whose matriarch freezes it and sends it to her daughters across the country.

7 or 8 New Mexico green chiles

1 tablespoon extra-virgin olive oil

2 cups cubed boneless pork, or protein of choice

1 medium onion, diced

3 or 4 garlic cloves, diced

3 tablespoons all-purpose flour

4 to 5 cups stock of choice (page xv), or water

2 teaspoons onion powder

2 teaspoons garlic powder

2 teaspoons salt

1. Preheat the oven to 350°F.

2. Spread the chiles on a baking sheet, and roast for 10 minutes. Or roast over a low flame on a grill for 15 to 20 minutes, flipping occasionally, until the skin is blackened. Place in a sealed container for 30 minutes while they cool. Then peel and dice.

3. In a large skillet over medium heat, cook the pork in the olive oil until browned, about 7 minutes. Add the onion and garlic, and cook until the onions are translucent, about 4 minutes. Add the chiles and cook for about 5 minutes, stirring often. Add the flour and cook, stirring constantly, to brown (but not burn!).

4. When the flour is browned and the protein is evenly coated, add the water, bring to a boil, and stir in the onion and garlic powders and salt. Cover and simmer on low for about 2 hours.

STORAGE: *4 days in the refrigerator, in a glass jar or plastic container, or a few months in the freezer in a plastic freezer bag or container*

REPURPOSING TIP: *Add this sauce to soups or stews to create a dynamic dish filled with spice and everything nice.*

PAIRINGS AND
SERVING IDEAS

MAINS

Sautéed
Thin-Cut Pork
Chops (page 146)

Turkey Breast
Scaloppini Style
(page 148)

Pan-Seared
Boneless Chicken
Thighs (page 149)

Vegetable
Stir-Fry (page 169)

Pan-Roasted
Veggies (page 171)

Tacos

Enchiladas

SIDES

Black Beans and
Wild Rice (page 186)

Hominy

Spanish rice

Tortillas

Arepas

Butternut-Beet Sauce //

SOUTHWESTERN SQUASH SAUCE

DAIRY FREE • GLUTEN FREE • NUT FREE • VEGAN

PREP TIME:
10 MINUTES,
PLUS 20 MINUTES
TO SOAK

COOK TIME:
20 MINUTES

MAKES:
ABOUT 3½ TO
4 CUPS

FLAVOR NOTES

SMOKY

WARM

FRESH

VIVID

HEAT INDEX

TYPE OF SAUCE

POUR OVER

MIX IN

SPREAD

This squash sauce, inspired by and with the blessing of Diné chef Brian Yazzie, combines several American ingredients that pair with almost any base, such is their resourcefulness. Squash, allspice, and chiles are all native to the Americas. Brian's work in the decolonization of food movement celebrates Native ingredients and informs us on how we can build more sustainable eating practices. If local components are the next natural progression of food preparation, recipes like this are good ones to know.

2 dried ancho chiles, stemmed and seeded

3 tablespoons extra-virgin olive oil

3 cups (1 pound) peeled, seeded, and cubed butternut squash

1 cup (¼ pound) peeled and cubed beets

1 teaspoon ground allspice

2 shallots, diced

1 overripe banana, mashed

2 tablespoons unfiltered apple cider vinegar

2 teaspoons salt

1 fresh sage sprig, or about 4 to 5 leaves

SPECIAL EQUIPMENT NEEDED

Food processor

1. Soak the chiles in a small bowl of warm water for 20 minutes. Drain the water into a small bowl, and set aside the chiles and water separately.

2. In a large, deep pan or Dutch oven over medium heat, mix the oil with the squash, beets, and allspice. Cover and cook for 10 minutes, until the squash begins to soften.

3. Add the shallots, banana, and chiles, then mix in the vinegar. Cook for another 10 minutes over medium-low heat, until the shallots are translucent, stirring constantly.

4. Transfer to a food processor. Add the salt and sage, and pulse to desired consistency. Add some chili water (about ½ cup) to thin, if necessary.

STORAGE: *1 to 2 weeks in the refrigerator, in a glass jar or plastic container*

REPURPOSING TIP: *Add hot chicken or vegetable stock to the finished sauce to make this more of a soup.*

PAIRINGS AND
SERVING IDEAS

MAINS

Pan-Seared
Crispy-Skin Duck
Breast (page 150)

Pan-Seared
Boneless Chicken
Thighs (page 149)

Grilled Salmon
(page 156)

Baked Salmon
(page 156)

Hand-Rolled
Gnocchi (page 187)

SIDES

Pan-Roasted
Veggies (page 171)

Hand-Cut Zucchini
Noodles (page 174)

Mojito // MOJO SAUCE

DAIRY FREE • GLUTEN FREE • NUT FREE • VEGAN

PREP TIME:
10 MINUTES

COOK TIME:
5 MINUTES

MAKES:
ABOUT 1 CUP

FLAVOR NOTES
ACIDIC
CITRUSY
TART
SPICY

HEAT INDEX

TYPE OF SAUCE
CONDIMENT
MARINADE
POUR OVER
COOK IN

Cuban cuisine has been close to my heart ever since my college roommate invited me to her home in Miami and introduced me to her mom's wonderful Cuban food. It's fair to note that there is a difference between plates on the resource-deprived island after a devastating embargo and those of the Cuban diaspora in south Florida. However, what both share is the soul of food that is created to be shared and enjoyed with family. The Vadia clan, which was my surrogate family for two years, is the inspiration for this mojo recipe. If you're using this as a marinade for fish, don't let it sit too long; 1 to 2 hours is appropriate.

3 garlic cloves, unpeeled

Salt

Freshly ground black pepper

2 tablespoons light oil (olive, grapeseed, vegetable, or avocado)

1 shallot, finely minced

1 green chile pepper (jalapeño or small Anaheim), finely minced

¾ cup sour orange juice (see Ingredient tip)

SPECIAL EQUIPMENT NEEDED

Mortar and pestle

1. In a small skillet over medium heat, dry roast the garlic cloves in their husks for 3 to 5 minutes. Let cool, peel, and finely mince them.

2. In the mortar, grind the garlic, and add pinch each of salt and pepper.

3. In a large bowl, combine the garlic with the oil, shallot, chile pepper, and orange juice. Whisk until the sauce comes together.

STORAGE: *5 days in the refrigerator in a glass jar or plastic container, or 2 months in the freezer in a plastic freezer bag or container*

INGREDIENT TIP: *Sour oranges can be hard to find; you can use ½ cup orange juice and ¼ cup lime juice instead.*

PAIRINGS AND
SERVING IDEAS

MAINS

Sautéed
Thin-Cut Pork
Chops (page 146)

Pan-Seared Sea
Scallops (page 165)

Pan-Seared White
Fish (page 161)

Turkey Breast
Scaloppini Style
(page 148)

SIDES

Bell Pepper Egg
Boats (page 172)

Duck Fat Fries
(page 176)

Black Beans and
Wild Rice (page 186)

Fried yucca

Arepas

Tortillas

Jerk "Store" Sauce //

SMOKY HOT BBQ SAUCE

DAIRY FREE • NUT FREE • VEGETARIAN

PREP TIME:
10 MINUTES,
PLUS 10 MINUTES
TO COOL

COOK TIME:
25 MINUTES

MAKES:
ABOUT 2 CUPS

FLAVOR NOTES
SPICY
HOT
SWEET
WARM

HEAT INDEX

TYPE OF SAUCE
CONDIMENT
MARINADE
POUR OVER
COOK IN

The balance of tangy sweet and spicy heat makes jerk tick. I love it as a paste and marinade, too, but it is easily converted to a sauce. I offered my neighbor in New Orleans some jerk chicken from the recipe in Spices, and she politely declined given the heat, giving it out to family instead. Later, she returned the container and told me it was delicious. When I asked her about it, she said matter-of-factly, "That wasn't hot at all, baby." That I had put three habaneros in there didn't seem to move the needle for Mrs. Frances, so notch up the heat by throwing in a couple extra chiles if you have a higher tolerance. Here's how to turn jerk into a versatile barbecue sauce. Leave out the stock or water if you want it more like a paste.

6 teaspoons coconut
oil, divided

1 shallot, chopped

2 scallions, green parts
only, chopped

2 garlic cloves, minced

3 Scotch bonnet or habanero
chiles, stemmed and seeded
(see Ingredient tip)

¼ cup tomato paste

½ cup chicken or vegetable
stock (page xv), or water

2 teaspoons ground allspice

½ cup fresh pineapple chunks

2 tablespoons soy sauce

¼ cup apple cider vinegar

¼ cup brown sugar

1 teaspoon salt

2 tablespoons honey

Juice and zest of 1 lime

SPECIAL EQUIPMENT NEEDED

Food processor

1. In a medium skillet over medium heat, heat 2 teaspoons of oil. When hot, add the shallot, scallions, garlic, and chiles, and sauté until golden, 4 to 5 minutes.

2. Add the tomato paste and stock. Mix and cook until everything comes together, about 5 minutes.

3. Mix in the allspice, pineapple, soy sauce, vinegar, sugar, and salt. Stir. Then turn off the heat and let cool for 10 minutes.

4. Transfer to a food processor, and pulse until combined and a paste is formed.

5. Return the mixture to the skillet. Add the honey and lime juice and zest. Cook over low heat, reducing, for 15 minutes.

6. To use as a cook-in sauce, use half the sauce to cook 4 to 6 pieces of your chosen base, and save the rest to pour over when it's done cooking.

STORAGE: *1 to 2 weeks in the refrigerator, in a glass jar or plastic container*

INGREDIENT TIP: *The heat in this recipe is entirely under your control. Remove the seeds and use fewer chiles to reduce the heat. Keep the seeds and add more chiles to induce it. The more often you eat a spice, the more tolerant you will become.*

PAIRINGS AND
SERVING IDEAS

MAINS

**Sautéed
Thin-Cut Pork
Chops (page 146)**

**Skirt Steak a la
Parrilla (page 144)**

**Pan-Seared
Boneless Chicken
Thighs (page 149)**

**Sautéed Shrimp
(page 164)**

SIDES

**Black Beans and
Wild Rice (page 186)**

White rice

Arepas

Mole Poblano de mi Abuelo //

CHILI AND CHOCOLATE SAUCE

DAIRY FREE

PREP TIME:
45 MINUTES

COOK TIME:
1 ½ HOURS

MAKES:
5 CUPS

FLAVOR NOTES
SPICY
SWEET
WARM
HOT

HEAT INDEX

TYPE OF SAUCE
COOK IN
POUR OVER

*M*ole melts the heart quicker than it melts the famous piece of chocolate one adds at the end. It derives from the Aztec Nahuatl word molli—roughly "a sauce made with chiles" or "a mixture." The sauce originates from the Mexican states of Puebla and Oaxaca. It has many editions of varying complexity, with some involving more than 20 ingredients. This recipe, from my dear friend Lola Lozano Lara's grandfather, Papa Lara (who is from Veracruz), oozes versatility and simplicity (by mole standards).

3½ ounces dried ancho chiles (about 10; see Ingredient tip)

3½ ounces dried mulato chiles (about 20; see Ingredient tip)

1¾ ounces dried pasilla chiles (about 5; see Ingredient tip)

1 bolillo bread roll, or 6 or 7 white bread slices, crusts removed, torn into pieces

1 corn tortilla, torn into pieces

⅓ cup raisins

2 tablespoons crushed almonds

1 teaspoon sesame seeds

6 peppercorns

5 cloves

1 cinnamon stick

1 tablespoon vegetable oil

½ medium onion, chopped

½ very ripe plantain, sliced

1 teaspoon salt

1½ ounces Mexican chocolate or dark baking chocolate (vegan and more than 70% cacao), divided

2 cups chicken or vegetable stock, divided (page xv)

SPECIAL EQUIPMENT NEEDED

Spice grinder or mortar and pestle, large cast iron pan or Dutch oven, food processor or blender

1. Remove the veins and seeds from all the chiles. In a large braising pan over low heat, toast all the chiles for 5 to 8 minutes to release their flavors. Add water to the pan so it just covers the chiles.

2. Add the bread, tortilla, raisins, and almonds. Turn the heat down very low and let soak for 30 minutes. Drain the excess water into a bowl and set aside for adding to the sauce as it cooks down.

3. In a small skillet over low heat, roast the sesame seeds, peppercorns, cloves, and cinnamon stick for 2 to 3 minutes. Set aside to cool, then grind each separately in a mortar and pestle or together in a spice grinder.

4. In your large cast iron pan, heat the oil over medium-low heat. Sauté the onion until golden brown, about 5 minutes.

5. Transfer the drained chili mixture to a food processor or blender. Add the onions and the plantain. Process until combined, adding a splash of the chili water if necessary.

6. Return everything to the cast iron pan. Over low to medium heat, mix in the ground spices, salt, and about half of the chocolate along with 1 cup of stock. Let the mole cook down for 30 minutes.

7. Add your protein of choice. Turn the protein every so often until cooked through, roughly 30 minutes for chicken. Use the remaining 1 cup of stock and, if needed, some of the chili water to keep it moist as the sauce cooks down.

STORAGE: *1 week in the refrigerator in a glass jar or plastic container (although it might stain) or 1 month in the freezer in a plastic freezer bag or container*

INGREDIENT TIP: *Chipotle, morita, and guajillo chiles are recommendations for substitutes. Be careful as you work with them, and don't touch your eyes. It's best to use gloves.*

PAIRINGS AND
SERVING IDEAS

MAINS

Sautéed
Thin-Cut Pork
Chops (page 146)

Stovetop Lamb Loin
Chops (page 147)

Pan-Seared
Boneless Chicken
Thighs (page 149)

Turkey Breast
Scaloppini Style
(page 148)

SIDES

Bell Pepper Egg
Boats (page 172)

Rice

Arepas

Tortillas (soft corn
ones are traditional)

Tomatillo Salsa Verde //

GREEN SALSA

DAIRY FREE • GLUTEN FREE • NUT FREE • VEGAN

PREP TIME:
20 MINUTES

COOK TIME:
20 MINUTES

MAKES:
ABOUT 2½ TO
3½ CUPS

FLAVOR NOTES
TANGY
BOTANICAL
MUSKY
TART

HEAT INDEX

TYPE OF SAUCE
CONDIMENT
MIX IN
POUR OVER

Tomatillos are secretly the next culinary thing. Shhh—don't tell anyone. They are an extremely versatile nightshade, often called husk tomatoes in the United States. Picked early, they're a perfect base for a tart salsa. Harvested late, they're a hearty tomato substitute. Notoriously disease resistant, they may just be the crop of the future. I owe my tomatillo inspiration to Eddie Hernandez, author of Turnip Greens and Tortillas and owner of Taqueria del Sol in Georgia and Tennessee. His paired-back use of them unlocked the secret to their potential: keep it simple.

3 tablespoons extra-virgin olive oil, divided

1 pound (about 16) ripe tomatillos, husked

2 chipotle chiles in adobo

½ green bell pepper, diced

½ red bell pepper, diced

2 shallots, chopped

5 garlic cloves, sliced

1 teaspoon ground cumin

1 teaspoon ground coriander

Salt

1 small bunch fresh parsley, chopped

2 scallions, green parts only, chopped

1 small handful pine nuts, crushed

SPECIAL EQUIPMENT NEEDED

Food processor

1. In a large braisier or heavy covered skillet over medium heat, heat 2 tablespoons of olive oil. Add the tomatillos and fry for about 10 to 15 minutes, rotating occasionally, until soft and a little charred on all sides.

2. In a medium pan over medium heat, heat the remaining tablespoon of olive oil. Add the chipotle chiles, green and red peppers, shallots, and garlic, and sauté until the shallots turn golden brown, about 5 minutes. Mix in the cumin and coriander and a healthy pinch of salt.

3. In the food processor, combine the pepper mixture with the softened tomatillos, and pulse or use the chop setting.

4. Transfer to a bowl. Garnish with the parsley, scallions, and pine nuts, and season with salt.

STORAGE: *1 week in the refrigerator in a glass jar or plastic container or 1 month in the freezer in a plastic freezer bag or container*

REPURPOSING TIP: *Use this hot on pasta or cooked meat, or let cool for a divine salsa. Throw in a couple of chopped tomatoes or 4 ounces of tomato paste with a little cream to make a more robust pasta sauce.*

PAIRINGS AND
SERVING IDEAS

MAINS

Sautéed
Thin-Cut Pork
Chops (page 146)

Pan-Seared
Boneless Chicken
Thighs (page 149)

Baked White
Fish (page 160)

Stovetop Mussels
(page 162)

SIDES

Bell Pepper Egg
Boats (page 172)

Black Beans and
Wild Rice (page 186)

Baked beans

Arepas

Tortillas

Guasacaca // CHUNKY AVOCADO SAUCE

DAIRY FREE • GLUTEN FREE • NUT FREE • VEGAN

PREP TIME:
15 MINUTES

MAKES:
ABOUT 2 CUPS

FLAVOR NOTES

BOTANICAL

MILD

PINEY

FRESH

HEAT INDEX

TYPE OF SAUCE

CONDIMENT

DIPPING

G uasacaca—or wasacaca *(a slightly different Dominican sauce shares this name)*—is Venezuela's avocado-based accompaniment that is less like guacamole and more like the love child of guac and chimichurri. *It's made with a vinegar base instead of lime juice, which adds a savory deliciousness that I hope you'll recognize as the level the avocado sauces you've been eating have been lacking. This recipe was inspired by the sacred Venezuelan culinary text* Mi Cocina a la Manera de Caracas, *and so there are still chunky parts of avocado in the sauce. The health properties of avocado seeds are legendary. It won't help the taste, but try grating some seed into the sauce whenever you're using avocados.*

¼ cup tomatoes, peeled, seeded, and chopped

½ cup shallots, minced

¼ cup bell pepper, seeded, deveined, and minced

1 tablespoon chopped fresh parsley

1 to 2 garlic cloves, crushed

¼ cup white wine vinegar

1 teaspoon salt

Dash freshly ground black pepper

Dash hot sauce

¾ cup puréed avocado

¾ cup chopped avocado

1. In a large mixing bowl, combine the tomatoes, shallots, bell pepper, parsley, garlic, vinegar, salt, pepper, hot sauce, and avocado. Mash together with the back of a spoon until the consistency is even.

2. Keep in the fridge until ready to serve.

STORAGE: *1 week in the refrigerator in a glass jar (pour a thin layer of lemon juice on top to help preserve it)*

REPURPOSING TIP: *Combine this sauce on a salad with equal parts oil and balsamic vinegar for a salad dressing.*

PAIRINGS AND SERVING IDEAS

MAINS

Skirt Steak a la Parrilla (page 144)

Turkey Breast Scaloppini Style (page 148)

Pan-Seared Boneless Chicken Thighs (page 149)

White Fish in Parchment (page 158)

Baked White Fish (page 160)

Pan-Seared White Fish (page 161)

SIDES

Bell Pepper Egg Boats (page 172)

Black Beans and Wild Rice (page 186)

Mixed Green Salad (page 170)

Choripán (chorizo hand sandwiches)

Arepas

Tortillas

Salsa de Mani // PEANUT SAUCE

DAIRY FREE • GLUTEN FREE • VEGAN

PREP TIME:
10 MINUTES

COOK TIME:
30 MINUTES

MAKES:
ABOUT 4 CUPS

FLAVOR NOTES
FRUITY
SWEET
VIVID
EARTHY

TYPE OF SAUCE
MARINADE
COOK IN
MIX IN
BASE

*S*alsa de Mani is among South America's most
versatile, if not internationally recognized, sauces.
*You can roast and grind peanuts to make this the long
way, or shortcut by using peanut butter. What results is
a creamy sauce that is not limited to traditional potato
or yucca patties (called* llapingachos, *similar to arepas)
but is versatile enough for chicken, fries, pork, veggies, or
nearly all types of seafood. You can add a little ground
cumin and coriander to brighten up the sauce. Marcelo
Panta of Canoa in Ecuador was generous enough to teach
me how to make this sauce.*

1 large red onion,
   chopped, divided

½ tomato, chopped

2½ cups water

½ pound (about 1½ cups)
   peanuts, chopped, or ½ cup
   peanut butter

Salt

Freshly ground black pepper

1 tablespoon achiote oil
   (see Ingredient tip)

2 tablespoons extra-virgin
   olive oil

1 large bell pepper, any
   color, minced

2 tablespoons chopped fresh
   cilantro

SPECIAL EQUIPMENT NEEDED

Food processor or blender

1. In a medium saucepan, stir to combine half of the onion and the
tomato with the water. Bring to a boil. Boil over medium heat for
10 minutes, or until the onion is soft and the liquid thickens.

2. Transfer the vegetables to the blender or food processor, and mix in the peanuts. Season with salt and pepper.

3. Return the mixture to the saucepan, and bring to a boil again over low heat. Heat until desired consistency is achieved, somewhere between the thickness of ketchup or yogurt, about 15 to 20 minutes. Stir in the achiote oil.

4. In a large pan over medium-low heat, heat the olive oil. Add the other half of the onion and the bell pepper and lightly fry until the onions turn golden brown, about 5 minutes. Add the veggies to the mix, and stir.

5. Mix with the cilantro, and season with salt and pepper. Set aside to cool.

STORAGE: *1 week in the refrigerator in a glass jar or plastic container, or freeze in ice cube trays and keep 2 months in the freezer in a plastic freezer bag*

INGREDIENT TIP: *Make achiote oil by frying 1 tablespoon annatto seeds in ½ cup peanut oil for about 3 to 4 minutes. Strain out the seeds. Annatto (also called achiote) can be found in most Latin markets or ordered online.*

PAIRINGS AND
SERVING IDEAS

MAINS

Sautéed
Thin-Cut Pork
Chops (page 146)

Grilled
Flanken-Style
Ribs (page 143)

Pan-Seared
Boneless Chicken
Thighs (page 149)

Sautéed Shrimp
(page 164)

Pan-Seared Sea
Scallops (page 165)

SIDES

Black Beans and
Wild Rice (page 186)

Quinoa and Lentils
(page 183)

Calamari (squid)

Pebre // FRESH SALSA

DAIRY FREE • GLUTEN FREE • NUT FREE • VEGAN

PREP TIME:
15 MINUTES,
PLUS 30 MINUTES
TO BLEND

MAKES:
ABOUT 2½ CUPS

FLAVOR NOTES
TANGY
SAVORY
SPICY

HEAT INDEX
🌶🌶🌶🌶🌶

TYPE OF SAUCE
CONDIMENT
DIPPING

Pebre *is simply the most Chilean of sauces. There are two versions: One is heavy on the chili paste and lighter on the tomato, and this one is more like* pico de gallo *from Mexico or* vinaigrette *in Brazil. José Manuel Simián—whose Chilean roots run deep—calls pebre a state of mind, noting that how a Chilean prefers their pebre says a lot about them. Some like to (unjustly, according to him) soften the onion with water or skip the garlic. If you want to try replicating the Chilean experience, look for Portuguese rolls, as they are closest to* the marraqueta, *the Chilean version of the baguette. Slice them in half, toast them, add a little bit of butter, and then layer the pebre on top. Pebre is also part of a Chilean idiomatic expression: If someone "made pebre out of you," it means they beat you up. This recipe—an alternative to pico—is offered in peace.*

2 big, flavorful tomatoes, chopped into small cubes

½ white onion, chopped into small cubes

2 garlic cloves, chopped

1 fresh chile pepper, such as jalapeño, finely chopped

½ cup chopped fresh cilantro

1 tablespoon chili paste (optional)

Juice of ½ lemon

2 tablespoons extra-virgin olive oil

Salt

1. In a large bowl, mix together the tomatoes, onion, garlic, chile pepper, cilantro, chili paste, lemon juice, and olive oil, and season with salt.

2. Let rest for 30 minutes so the flavors can blend before serving.

STORAGE: *2 to 3 days in the refrigerator in a glass jar or plastic container, but best to use fresh*

REPURPOSING TIP: *You can add a squirt of white vinegar or white wine, or another spoonful of olive oil, if you want to tweak the flavor. Or add equal parts oil and vinegar to make a salad dressing.*

PAIRINGS AND
SERVING IDEAS

MAINS

Turkey Breast
Scaloppini Style
(page 148)

Pan-Seared
Boneless Chicken
Thighs (page 149)

Salmon in
Parchment
(page 155)

Grilled White
Fish (page 159)

Sautéed Shrimp
(page 164)

Stovetop Mussels
(page 162)

SIDES

Bell Pepper Egg
Boats (page 172)

Black Beans and
Wild Rice (page 186)

Choripán (chorizo
hand sandwiches)

Arepas

Tortillas

Chimichurri // GREEN HERB SAUCE

DAIRY FREE • GLUTEN FREE • NUT FREE • VEGAN

PREP TIME:
20 MINUTES,
PLUS OVERNIGHT
TO BLEND

COOK TIME:
5 MINUTES

MAKES:
ABOUT 2 CUPS

FLAVOR NOTES
HERBACEOUS
AROMATIC
FLORAL
COOLING

HEAT INDEX

TYPE OF SAUCE
CONDIMENT
MARINADE
MIX IN

*C*himichurri is a mainstay at my backyard *parrilladas. The South American green sauce can go on nearly anything that comes off the grill. The basic recipe uses parsley, oregano, oil, and red wine vinegar. However, it often isn't communicated how much gets added by proper execution and taking the time to hand chop the ingredients. Avoid a food processor on this one and meticulously cut the parsley yourself. This recipe comes from Petry Fernández Díaz, who runs the Buenos Aires-based barbecue company* Nice to Meat You.

4 or 5 whole garlic cloves, unpeeled

2 bunches fresh flat-leaf parsley (about 6 ounces total), stemmed and carefully minced

2 tablespoons minced fresh oregano or tarragon leaves

1 teaspoon crushed red pepper flakes

3 tablespoons red wine vinegar or sherry vinegar

1¼ cups extra-virgin olive oil

Coarse sea salt

Freshly ground black pepper

Juice and zest of 1 lemon

1 tablespoon sweet paprika

1. In a small skillet over medium heat, dry roast the garlic cloves in their husks for 2 to 3 minutes. Let cool, peel, and finely mince.

2. In a large bowl, combine the parsley, oregano, garlic, and red pepper flakes. Add the vinegar and oil, season with salt and pepper, and whisk in the lemon juice, lemon zest, and paprika.

3. Let rest at room temperature for 6 to 8 hours or overnight. Chimichurri is almost always better the next day.

STORAGE: *2 weeks in the refrigerator in a glass jar (it will turn plastic green)*

REPURPOSING TIP: *My mom puts a dash of anchovy paste in her Chimichurri—no regrets.*

PAIRINGS AND
SERVING IDEAS

MAINS

Skirt Steak a la
Parrilla (page 144)

Grilled
Flanken-Style
Ribs (page 143)

Pan-Seared
Boneless Chicken
Thighs (page 149)

Grilled Salmon
(page 156)

Stovetop Mussels
(page 162)

Pan-Seared Sea
Scallops (page 165)

SIDES

Bell Pepper Egg
Boats (page 172)

Black Beans and
Wild Rice (page 186)

Choripán (chorizo
hand sandwiches)

Bread

Salsa Criolla // BELL PEPPER SAUCE

DAIRY FREE • GLUTEN FREE • NUT FREE • VEGAN

PREP TIME:
10 MINUTES,
PLUS 30 MINUTES
TO BLEND

MAKES:
ABOUT 3 CUPS

FLAVOR NOTES
FLORAL
FRUITY
BOTANICAL
FRESH

TYPE OF SAUCE
CONDIMENT

Salsa Criolla has different versions, depending on which South American country you happen to be in. In Peru, for example, it's half-moon sliced onions in an acidic base. The type along the Mar de Plata in Argentina and Uruguay is this version. I prefer it. Since Uruguay is one of my favorite countries on the planet, I asked about a recipe from my half-Argentine, half-Uruguayan pal Carolina Moppett. She offered this family recipe, with the caveat that when her family makes it they just estimate the amounts.

1 yellow bell pepper, seeded and deveined, diced

1 red bell pepper, seeded and deveined, diced

6 tablespoons extra-virgin olive oil, divided

1 tomato, minced

1 onion, minced

2 tablespoons apple cider vinegar

1 teaspoon dried oregano

Salt

Freshly ground black pepper

1. In a large mixing bowl, combine the bell peppers, olive oil, tomato, onion, vinegar, and oregano, and season with salt and pepper.

2. Let rest for 30 minutes before serving to allow the flavors to blend.

STORAGE: *3 to 4 days in the refrigerator in a glass jar, but best to use fresh*

PAIRINGS AND
SERVING IDEAS

MAINS

Grilled
Flanken-Style
Ribs (page 143)

Skirt Steak a la
Parrilla (page 144)

Sautéed
Thin-Cut Pork
Chops (page 146)

Stovetop Lamb Loin
Chops (page 147)

Pan-Seared
Boneless Chicken
Thighs (page 149)

Pan-Seared
Crispy-Skin Duck
Breast (page 150)

Pan-Seared White
Fish (page 161)

SIDES

Smashed Garlic Red
Potatoes (page 176)

Black Beans and
Wild Rice (page 186)

Choripán (chorizo
hand sandwiches)

3

MIDDLE EAST, AFRICA, EASTERN MEDITERRANEAN, AND CAUCASUS

THIS CHAPTER STRETCHES FROM THE EASTERN Mediterranean and the Caucasus south through the Middle East and then into Africa. The diversity of culture and geography is reflected in the sauces curated for this chapter. Not that there aren't common flavors and ingredients: Garlic, cilantro, parsley, chiles, tomatoes, and bell peppers are interwoven. However, this chapter begins with a tart, sweet Georgian plum sauce (page 74) and ends with a funky South African barbecue sauce evocatively named Monkey Gland Sauce (page 102), which contains zero guts of primates but might be the tangiest version of barbecue sauce on the planet.

In between, you may notice some familiar names, and some sauces you may be more acquainted with than you realize. Baba Ghanoush (page 84) has an international presence. Harissa (page 92) and Chermoula (page 90) do as well, though in this book, you'll find they have switched colors to reflect regional differences.

Haydari and Cacik (page 76), relatives of the Greek tzatziki, represent the classic yogurt dipping sauce. Jajik (page 80) is another member of the family—an Assyrian dairy-based sauce that is perfect as part of a meze tray (think: appetizer) with some of the other recipes in this section: Baba Ghanoush, Hummus (page 86), Toum (page 94), Zhoug (page 96).... Make them all! Muhammara (page 78), like the Jajik recipe, was generously provided by Kathryn Pauline of *Cardamom and Tea*, which happens to be just the loveliest Assyrian food blog on the Internet.

Middle East and North African (known as MENA) cuisine is my jam. Full stop. So I appealed to *Spices* contributor Beeta Mohajeri to share her mother's pomegranate stew sauce, Khoresh Fesenjoon (page 82). For this sauce (and for several in this section) you'll need to get your hands on pomegranate molasses. Its tart sweetness is a peerless culinary tool.

Though you may not be familiar with every sauce or every name, you'll find the recipes easy to learn and relatively simple to make and use. More than that, most of them are effortless to share. Whether it's in mezes or as part of larger shared main plates, using food to make that connection with folks is why this chapter stands out, and why I hope it is the most used chapter of the book.

Tkemali // PLUM SAUCE

DAIRY FREE • GLUTEN FREE • NUT FREE • VEGAN

PREP TIME:
5 MINUTES

COOK TIME:
55 MINUTES

MAKES:
ABOUT 1 TO
2 CUPS

FLAVOR NOTES
TART
SOUR
SWEET

HEAT INDEX

TYPE OF SAUCE
CONDIMENT
POUR OVER

Tkemali *is a tart plum sauce made from a green cherry plum called* alycha, *though different types can be used to vary the color and sweetness. This recipe comes from Margarita Gerliani, whose dad is from Svaneti, in the north of Georgia high in the mountains. They use utskho suneli (blue fenugreek), an herb that grows wild in the mountainous parts of northern Georgian. Another ingredient, Svanuri marili—a spiced salt—originates from the same region. Margarita told me Tkemali sauce goes best with shashlik and lyulya kebabs (think shish kebabs) or fish. It also works as a salad dressing. Adding the plum water at the end helps make it a thin sauce, but if you want it a bit thicker, try cooking it down or even adding a bit of cornstarch.*

1 pound green cherry plums or seasonal plums of your choice

1 tablespoon chopped fresh cilantro

1 teaspoon ground coriander

3 garlic cloves, minced

1 teaspoon hot paprika

2 teaspoons Svanuri marili (see Ingredient tip)

1 teaspoon dried blue fenugreek (see Ingredient tip)

Sugar (optional)

Salt

SPECIAL EQUIPMENT NEEDED

Food processor or mortar and pestle

1. Put the cherry plums in a medium saucepan, add cold water to the top of the pan, and bring to a boil over medium heat. Cover and cook until the plums are very soft, about 15 minutes (depending on the variety of plums). Set aside to cool. Pour the water from the cooked plums into a bowl and reserve.

2. Strain the plums through a colander to separate the stones and skin from the pulp. Push the flesh with the back of a wooden spoon to get the most pulp you can. Transfer the flesh to the saucepan.

3. In a small bowl, combine the cilantro, coriander, garlic, paprika, Svanuri marili, and blue fenugreek. Then grind them with the help of a mortar and pestle or a food processor.

4. Add the spice mixture to the pan with the plum pulp. Cook over low heat for 30 to 40 minutes, until you have a thick sauce. Stir in some of the reserved plum water to make a thinner sauce.

5. Stir in the sugar, if using, and season with salt.

STORAGE: *2 to 4 days in the refrigerator in a glass jar or plastic container, or 2 to 3 months frozen in a plastic container*

INGREDIENT TIP: *Svanuri marili (Svaneti salt) is a seasoning mixture made of spices, garlic, and salt. If you can't find it online, use crushed garlic, black pepper, coriander, crushed red pepper flakes and salt in equal parts. Blue fenugreek is an herb that is not easily replicated but can be found easily online. About 5 ground fenugreek seeds is a substitute for 1 teaspoon blue fenugreek, if needed.*

PAIRINGS AND
SERVING IDEAS

MAINS

Stovetop Lamb Loin Chops (page 147)

Turkey Breast Scaloppini Style (page 148)

Pan-Seared Boneless Chicken Thighs (page 149)

Salmon in Parchment (page 155)

White Fish in Parchment (page 158)

Pan-Seared Sea Scallops (page 165)

Kebabs

Burgers

SIDES

Vegetable Stir-Fry (page 169)

Pan-Roasted Veggies (page 171)

Smashed Garlic Red Potatoes (page 176)

Roasted Fingerling Potatoes (page 177)

Haydari and Cacik // YOGURT DIP

GLUTEN FREE • NUT FREE • VEGETARIAN

PREP TIME:
5 MINUTES,
PLUS OVERNIGHT
TO DRAIN AND
1 HOUR TO SIT

MAKES:
ABOUT 2 TO
3 CUPS

FLAVOR NOTES

CREAMY
REFRESHING
COOLING
FRESH

TYPE OF SAUCE

CONDIMENT
DIPPING
SPREAD

Like Creole Remoulade and Comeback Sauce (page 46), Haydari *and* Cacik *are relatives, and both can easily be made from almost the same ingredients. Haydari is a bit thicker and doesn't usually contain cucumbers. Cacik does, and the viscosity ranges from a Jajik (page 80) to more like a cold soup. This recipe is for a thicker version of both sauces, which are ideal in a meze (appetizer platter), to share with many other sauces and snacks. Sumac is a tangy dried berry that is usually sold ground. Find it in the spice aisle or online. I owe a debt of gratitude to Beril Guceri and her Turkish mother Semra for their consult.*

2 cups full-fat plain yogurt (or 1½ cups Greek yogurt and skip step 1)

2 cucumbers, diced (optional for Cacik)

Salt

3 garlic cloves, minced

2 tablespoons extra-virgin olive oil

3 tablespoons grated feta cheese

2 tablespoons chopped fresh dill

1 tablespoon freshly squeezed lemon juice

1 teaspoon ground sumac

¼ cup chopped walnuts (optional for Haydari; omit for Nut Free)

SPECIAL EQUIPMENT NEEDED

Cheesecloth, mortar and pestle (or a spoon or knife)

1. Line a colander with a couple of layers of cheesecloth. Pour in the yogurt, and cover with plastic wrap. Let drain for several hours or overnight in the refrigerator.

2. If you're using the cucumber, put it in a medium bowl and toss with a small handful of salt. Let sit for 30 minutes to an hour. Drain and rinse the cucumbers, pat dry, and set aside.

3. In your mortar and pestle, or with the back of a spoon or side of a knife, crush the garlic into a finer paste.

4. In a large bowl, mix the oil and yogurt. Add the garlic, and season with salt. Add the feta, dill, lemon juice, sumac, and walnuts (if using), and stir.

5. Add the cucumbers from step 2, if using, and mix. Let rest for several minutes before serving.

STORAGE: *2 to 4 days in the refrigerator in a glass jar or plastic container*

INGREDIENT TIP: *High-quality feta and yogurt or* labneh *(cheese made from strained yogurt) make a huge difference. While not traditional, adding a bit of softened cream cheese can smooth both sauces out, or thicken if they're watery. If you can find goat or sheep's strained yogurt, try using that. It is thick like Greek yogurt (so you can skip step 1) and is sometimes available at Middle Eastern specialty shops.*

PAIRINGS AND
SERVING IDEAS

MAINS

Grilled
Flanken-Style
Ribs (page 143)

Skirt Steak a la
Parrilla (page 144)

Pan-Seared
Boneless Chicken
Thighs (page 149)

Kebabs

SIDES

Bell Pepper Egg
Boats (page 172)

Pan-Roasted
Veggies (page 171)

Potatoes Four
Ways (page 175)

Fluffy Couscous
(page 181)

Quinoa and Lentils
(page 183)

Charcuterie and
cheese plate

Falafel

Pita

Muhammara // BELL PEPPER SPREAD

DAIRY FREE • VEGAN

PREP TIME:
15 MINUTES,
PLUS 30 MINUTES
TO SWEAT

COOK TIME:
15 MINUTES

MAKES:
1½ CUPS

FLAVOR NOTES
SWEET
SOUR
SMOKY
SPICY

HEAT INDEX

TYPE OF SAUCE
SPREAD
CONDIMENT
POUR OVER
MIX IN

Muhammar *means "reddened" in Arabic, which is no surprise when you take a look at the ingredients list. The dish is made up mostly of charred red bell peppers flavored with deep red pomegranate molasses and intensified with a bit of crushed red pepper flakes. Look for deeply red bell peppers for a bright and flavorful final product. Kathryn Pauline, who writes the blog* Cardamom and Tea, *is a virtuoso of Assyrian cuisine. She shared this recipe with the assurance that Muhammara packs a punch and can be used to add a little sweet and sour to just about any weeknight meal.*

3 small red bell peppers

¼ cup finely chopped walnuts

¼ cup plain breadcrumbs

½ teaspoon ground cumin

1 small garlic clove, minced

2 tablespoons pomegranate
    molasses (see Ingredient tip)

Crushed red pepper flakes

½ teaspoon salt

Extra-virgin olive oil,
    for serving

SPECIAL EQUIPMENT NEEDED

Food processor

1. Place the red peppers directly over the flame of a gas burner on medium-high heat. Use tongs to rotate them until they're charred all over on the outside, roughly 8 minutes. (If you don't have a gas stove, broil the peppers on the highest setting or use an outdoor grill.) Place in a small bowl and cover with plastic wrap to sweat them for 30 minutes.

2. Place a medium skillet over medium heat for a minute. Once heated, add the walnuts and breadcrumbs. Stir as you cook for 5 minutes or so, until the aroma is toasty and everything begins to brown. Stir in the cumin and garlic in the final minute, and set aside.

3. Remove the skins of the peppers with your hands or a paper towel. Pat dry and discard the seeds, ribs, stems, and liquid.

4. Place the peppers in the food processor and mix. Add the walnut mixture, pomegranate molasses, crushed red pepper flakes, and salt, and pulse until it becomes a mostly smooth paste but with small chunks.

5. Transfer to a bowl, drizzle with olive oil, and serve.

STORAGE: *4 to 5 days in the refrigerator in a glass jar or plastic container, or freeze in tablespoon-size chunks on parchment paper and then keep for up to 3 months in a freezer bag*

INGREDIENT TIP: *Pomegranate molasses is the essential ingredient. A supermarket with a good international section, world markets, and Asian markets should have it. You'll also find it online.*

REPURPOSING TIP: *Manakish muhammara is a wonderful bread you can make with this recipe and pizza dough. Roll the dough out as you would to make little 8-inch pizzas, and top each with a layer of muhammara. Then bake on a preheated pizza stone at 450°F for 5 to 10 minutes.*

PAIRINGS AND
SERVING IDEAS

MAINS

Skirt Steak a la
Parrilla (page 144)

Grilled
Flanken-Style
Ribs (page 143)

Turkey Breast
Scaloppini Style
(page 148)

Pan-Seared
Boneless Chicken
Thighs (page 149)

Stovetop Mussels
(page 162)

SIDES

Potatoes Four
Ways (page 175)

Fluffy Couscous
(page 181)

Black Beans and
Wild Rice (page 186)

Quinoa and Lentils
(page 183)

Mezze with a variety
of dips and spreads

Jajik // ASSYRIAN DAIRY DIP

GLUTEN FREE • NUT FREE • VEGETARIAN

PREP TIME:
10 MINUTES

MAKES:
3 CUPS

FLAVOR NOTES
RICH
HERBY
CREAMY

TYPE OF SAUCE
DIPPING
CONDIMENT

Jajik *is a dairy-based dip from Iraq. It's often eaten for breakfast, but can also be part of a meze tray, along with other classics like Baba Ghanoush (page 84) and Hummus (page 86) and some bread. This is an adaptation of Kathryn Pauline's family's Assyrian version, with a cottage cheese and cream cheese base flavored with dill. But it's also delicious made with labneh (a soft cheese made from strained yogurt) and can include banana peppers, parsley, mint, garlic, and grated cucumber, or use whatever herbs you have on hand. Make sure you add the ingredients in the right order. If you add the herbs too early, or if you don't mix them in carefully, the whole thing will turn green. Also make sure you wash and dry your herbs before chopping, which will make the Jajik stay fresher, and will also keep it from turning green.*

8 ounces cream cheese, at room temperature

3 tablespoons unsalted butter, at room temperature

1 pound small curd cottage cheese

¼ teaspoon salt

3 tablespoons chopped fresh dill

3 tablespoons chopped fresh cilantro

2 tablespoons chopped scallions, green parts only

Extra-virgin olive oil, for garnish

Chopped fresh herbs, for garnish

1. In a medium mixing bowl, mix the cream cheese and butter together. Mix in the cottage cheese, and stir until everything is very evenly mixed together. Season with the salt.

2. Carefully fold in the dill, cilantro, and scallions.

3. When everything is evenly combined, store in the refrigerator for later, or serve right away. To serve, spoon into a serving bowl, drizzle with extra-virgin olive oil, and garnish with the fresh herbs.

STORAGE: *4 to 5 days in the refrigerator in a glass jar or plastic container*

REPURPOSING TIP: *Most traditionally, Jajik is not really used as a sauce for proteins. But less traditionally, it's really delicious served alongside roast chicken, and it goes wonderfully with beans and legumes, especially fava beans.*

PAIRINGS AND
SERVING IDEAS

MAINS

Stovetop Lamb Loin
Chops (page 147)

Skirt Steak a la
Parrilla (page 144)

Pan-Seared
Boneless Chicken
Thighs (page 149)

Turkey Breast
Scaloppini Style
(page 148)

SIDES

Bell Pepper Egg
Boats (page 172)

Pan-Roasted
Veggies (page 171)

Potatoes Four
Ways (page 175)

Fluffy Couscous
(page 181)

Quinoa and Lentils
(page 183)

Charcuterie and
cheese plates

Falafel

Olives

Pita

Khoresh Fesenjoon //

PERSIAN POMEGRANATE STEW

DAIRY FREE • GLUTEN FREE

PREP TIME:
30 MINUTES

COOK TIME:
1 HOUR
50 MINUTES

MAKES:
ABOUT 4 TO
5 CUPS

FLAVOR NOTES
SWEET
SOUR
TANGY
WARM

HEAT INDEX

TYPE OF SAUCE
COOK IN

Khoresh Fesenjoon, *informally known as* fesenjan *or* fessenjoon, *is a wonderfully tart Persian pomegranate stew. While it is commonly a sauce for chicken, regional differences and possible variants include lamb, duck (for special occasions), or vegetarian options like squash or eggplant. Beeta Mohajeri, an old friend and dynamic private chef, offered this recipe from her mother, Mama Fariba. I'm told Persian mothers make a big batch and freeze to use when desired. You can do the same. Serve over saffron rice.*

5 tablespoons butter or coconut oil (for Dairy Free)

2 large onions, thinly sliced

1 teaspoon salt

2 pounds boneless chicken thighs, cubed, or stew ingredients of your choice

½ pound shelled walnuts

½ cup pomegranate molasses dissolved in 2 cups water

½ teaspoon ground cinnamon

¼ teaspoon ground saffron dissolved in 1 tablespoon hot water

2 tablespoons sugar, as needed

Pomegranate seeds (optional)

SPECIAL EQUIPMENT NEEDED

Food processor, large Dutch oven

1. In a large Dutch oven over medium heat, melt the butter. Add the onions and brown for 6 to 8 minutes, until golden and translucent. Add the salt.

2. Add the chicken thighs, and sear until golden brown, about 10 minutes.

3. In a food processor, grind the walnuts very fine, then add 2 cups of the diluted pomegranate water, the cinnamon, and the saffron water. Mix into a creamy paste.

4. If the pomegranate-walnut paste is too sour, add sugar to taste until you get a balanced sweet and sour flavor. Add more molasses to sour it, more sugar to sweeten.

5. Transfer the pomegranate-walnut paste to the Dutch oven. Cover and simmer for 1½ hours, stirring occasionally with a spoon to prevent the nut paste from burning on the bottom. If the stew is too thick, add warm water to thin it out.

6. Transfer the stew to an oven-proof casserole dish. Cover with foil and keep warm in a preheated oven until ready to serve. Garnish with pomegranate seeds just before serving for a lovely texture and appearance.

STORAGE: *1 week in the refrigerator in a glass jar, or several months in the freezer in a freezer bag*

REPURPOSING TIP: *Serve with Persian-style rice, jeweled with saffron water. Cook basmati rice according to the package. Scoop out ⅓ cup of cooked rice and set aside. Mix a small pinch of saffron with 2 tablespoons of warm water. Let it dissolve, then mix the saffron water into the reserved rice. It will turn a beautiful orange. Use this to top your basmati rice.*

PAIRINGS AND
SERVING IDEAS

MAINS

Stovetop Lamb Loin
Chops (page 147)

Pan-Seared
Boneless Chicken
Thighs (page 149)

Pan-Seared
Crispy-Skin Duck
Breast (page 150)

Ground beef

Meatballs

—

SIDES

Fluffy Couscous
(page 181)

Butternut squash

Eggplant

Basmati rice

Baba Ghanoush // SPICED EGGPLANT SPREAD

DAIRY FREE • GLUTEN FREE • NUT FREE • VEGAN

PREP TIME:
25 MINUTES

COOK TIME:
50 MINUTES

MAKES:
ABOUT 1 TO
1½ CUPS

FLAVOR NOTES

SMOKY

SAVORY

AROMATIC

EARTHY

TYPE OF SAUCE

SPREAD

DIPPING

CONDIMENT

Baba Ghanoush is a Middle Eastern eggplant dip and sauce that can be used as part of a meze or spooned over any number of dishes. This recipe comes from Maryanne Wageh Guirguis and is great with anything from couscous to shish kebabs. The simple way to cook the eggplant is by broiling it, but the more adventurous should turn it over the flame on a gas stove or grill to accentuate the smoky flavor it releases. Tahini is a paste made from ground sesame seeds. You'll find it in many supermarkets and online. It may look a little oily when you open the jar; just stir to incorporate any oil that's risen to the top.

1 large eggplant

¼ cup tahini, plus more as needed

3 garlic cloves, minced

¼ cup freshly squeezed lemon juice, plus more as needed

Pinch ground cumin

Salt

1 tablespoon extra-virgin olive oil

1 tablespoon chopped fresh flat-leaf parsley

¼ cup brine-cured black olives, such as Kalamata (optional)

1. Prepare a medium-hot fire in a charcoal grill and preheat the oven to 375°F.

2. Prick the eggplant with a fork in several places. To char on a charcoal grill, place on the grill rack 4 to 5 inches from the fire. Grill, turning frequently, until the skin blackens and blisters and the flesh just begins to feel soft, 10 to 15 minutes. To char in the broiler, roast the eggplant on an oiled baking sheet for 20 to 30 minutes. To char on a gas flame on the stovetop, hold over the flame with tongs. Rotate the eggplant repeatedly until the skin is papery and evenly charred.

3. Transfer the eggplant to a baking sheet and bake until very soft, 15 to 20 minutes. Remove from the oven, let cool slightly, and peel off and discard the skin.

4. Place the eggplant flesh in a medium bowl. Using a fork, mash the eggplant to a paste. Add the tahini, garlic, lemon juice, and cumin, and mix well. Season with salt, then taste and add more tahini and/or lemon juice, if needed.

5. Transfer the mixture to a serving bowl, and use the back of a spoon to form a shallow well. Drizzle the olive oil over the top, and sprinkle with the parsley. Place the olives around the sides (if using).

6. Serve at room temperature.

STORAGE: *6 days in the refrigerator in a glass jar or plastic container; freeze for 2 months by setting the Baba Ghanoush over cheesecloth in a colander and letting it drain for 30 minutes, then put in a freezer bag with the air squeezed out, or vacuum seal*

REPURPOSING TIP: *You can use this as a soup thickener, a salad dressing (perhaps with a little oil to thin it), or a sandwich spread.*

PAIRINGS AND
SERVING IDEAS

MAINS

Skirt Steak a la
Parrilla (page 144)

Turkey Breast
Scaloppini Style
(page 148)

Kebabs

Steak

Burgers

SIDES

Mixed Green
Salad (page 170)

Bell Pepper Egg
Boats (page 172)

Pan-Roasted
Veggies (page 171)

Fluffy Couscous
(page 181)

Quinoa and Lentils
(page 183)

Pita

Hummus bi Tahina //

GROUND CHICKPEA AND TAHINI SAUCE

DAIRY FREE • GLUTEN FREE • NUT FREE • VEGAN

PREP TIME:
15 MINUTES,
PLUS OVERNIGHT
TO SOAK

COOK TIME:
1 HOUR
30 MINUTES

MAKES:
ABOUT 2 CUPS

FLAVOR NOTES

NUTTY
FRESH
CREAMY
MILD

TYPE OF SAUCE

DIPPING
CONDIMENT
SPREAD

The word hummus derives from the Arabic word for chickpeas, which were cultivated in the Mediterranean and Middle East thousands of years ago. The exact origin of hummus is contested, but the earliest mentions date back to thirteenth-century Egypt. There is a vast difference between the hummus you get in tubs at the store and the hummus made at home by an expert with a mortar and pestle. This recipe, from Erene Mina, will teach you the basics of making a restaurant-quality hummus at home. It calls for cooking the chickpeas from scratch, but you can substitute a 15-ounce can of cooked chickpeas, drained and rinsed well, then start with step 3.

⅔ cup dried chickpeas

½ teaspoon baking soda

¼ cup water, divided, plus extra for thinning

3 tablespoons tahini

3 tablespoons freshly squeezed lemon juice

1 tablespoon white vinegar

2 small garlic cloves, minced

1 teaspoon ground cumin

Salt

2 tablespoons extra-virgin olive oil

1 tablespoon smoked paprika

SPECIAL EQUIPMENT NEEDED

Food processor

1. Soak the chickpeas overnight in enough cold water to cover by 2 to 3 inches, and stir in the baking soda (to help with digestion). If you did not start the night before, soak the chickpeas for an hour in hot water. Drain, and rinse the chickpeas thoroughly with cold water.

2. Place the chickpeas in a large pot, cover with cold water, and bring to a boil over high heat. Reduce the heat and simmer for 90 minutes, stirring and checking from time to time for doneness (you want them very tender). Drain well. If you have the patience, peel them from their skins.

3. In the food processor, combine the chickpeas and 2 tablespoons of water, and process, stopping and scraping down the sides and bottom of the bowl as needed. Add the tahini, lemon juice, vinegar, and 2 tablespoons of water, and mix until well incorporated and creamy. Add the garlic, cumin, and salt, and mix again.

4. If the mixture is too thick for your taste, mix in 2 more tablespoons of water. Taste to adjust the salt.

5. Serve drizzled with the olive oil and paprika.

STORAGE: *4 to 5 days in the refrigerator in a glass jar or plastic container, with a thin layer of olive oil on top, or 3 months in the freezer in a freezer bag or plastic container*

REPURPOSING TIP: *Use as a sandwich spread instead of mustard, mayonnaise, or peanut butter. Or change the flavor profile; hummus is an amazing vehicle for adding your favorite ingredients. Try mixing in ground chipotle chili pepper while processing. Or before serving, mix in whole pomegranate seeds or pine nuts.*

PAIRINGS AND SERVING IDEAS

MAINS

Turkey Breast Scaloppini Style (page 148)

White Fish in Parchment (page 158)

Salmon in Parchment (page 155)

Hand-Rolled Gnocchi (page 187)

Homemade Pasta Noodles (page 184)

Falafel

Grilled chicken

Grilled beef

SIDES

Bell Pepper Egg Boats (page 172)

Vegetable Stir-Fry (page 169)

Smashed Garlic Red Potatoes (page 176)

Fluffy Couscous (page 181)

Quinoa and Lentils (page 183)

Eggplant

Pita

Naan

Any flatbread

Filfel Chuma // GARLIC HOT SAUCE

DAIRY FREE · GLUTEN FREE · NUT FREE · VEGAN

PREP TIME:
5 MINUTES,
PLUS 20 MINUTES
TO SOAK

COOK TIME:
5 MINUTES

MAKES:
ABOUT 1 CUP

FLAVOR NOTES
GARLICKY
HERBACEOUS
SPICY
WARM

HEAT INDEX
🌶🌶🌶

TYPE OF SAUCE
CONDIMENT
DIPPING
SPREAD
COOK IN

Filfel Chuma *is used often as a condiment in Libyan-Jewish and Israeli cooking. It is essentially a garlic hot sauce that sort of represents a marriage between Toum (page 94) and Harissa (page 92). In fact, my pal Shawn Bunkheila mentioned that his family often uses the same ingredients and just calls it harissa. The street his Libyan father, Ghazi, grew up on had a large Jewish community who referred to it by the name listed,* Filfel Chuma. *This sauce is perfect for widespread use, especially for Americans. My mom, who is Italian, says Americans often overuse garlic when only a little is needed. So this sauce is for those who unapologetically slather as much garlic as possible onto foods, but who also love heat and spice. Use only fresh garlic, not sprouted or old garlic.*

2 dried ancho chiles or chile peppers of choice, stemmed and seeded

12 garlic cloves

2 teaspoons cumin seeds

1 teaspoon caraway seeds

½ cup grapeseed oil, divided

1 teaspoon ground cayenne pepper

1 tablespoon smoked paprika

Juice and zest of ½ lemon

1 teaspoon salt

SPECIAL EQUIPMENT NEEDED

Spice grinder or mortar and pestle, food processor

1. In a small bowl, cover the chiles with warm water to reconstitute. Soak for 20 to 30 minutes, then drain and pat dry.

2. Meanwhile, remove any green parts or stems from the garlic cloves by degerming them. Slice each clove in half lengthwise, then use your finger to take out the little stem in the middle of the garlic clove, as it's usually a bit sour, especially in old garlic.

3. In a small, dry pan over medium heat, toast the cumin and caraway seeds for 1 minute. Let cool, and grind in the spice grinder or mortar and pestle.

4. In a skillet over medium-low heat, heat 1 tablespoon of oil. Add the garlic, and sauté until aromatic and just starting to wilt and turn golden.

5. In a food processor, combine the chiles, garlic, toasted seeds, cayenne pepper, paprika, lemon juice, lemon zest, salt, and the remaining ¼ cup plus 3 tablespoons oil, and mix until smooth. Add extra oil if the sauce is too thick.

STORAGE: *1 week in the refrigerator in a glass jar or plastic container, but best to use fresh*

REPURPOSING TIP: *Mix Filfel Chuma into ground beef while you're making burger patties. Stir it into Greek yogurt to use as a condiment for red meat like ribs and lamb, or just for a creamier sauce.*

PAIRINGS AND
SERVING IDEAS

MAINS

Stovetop Lamb Loin
Chops (page 147)

Grilled Flanken-
Style Ribs
(page 143)

Pan-Seared
Boneless Chicken
Thighs (page 149)

Pan-Seared
Crispy-Skin Duck
Breast (page 150)

Pan-Seared White
Fish (page 161)

Pan-Seared Salmon
(page 157)

Sautéed Shrimp
(page 164)

Stovetop Mussels
(page 162)

SIDES

Pan-Roasted
Veggies (page 171)

Bell Pepper Egg
Boats (page 172)

Potatoes Four
Ways (page 175)

Fluffy Couscous
(page 181)

Quinoa and Lentils
(page 183)

Black Beans and
Wild Rice (page 186)

Grilled eggplant

Chermoula Rouge // SWEET RAISIN SAUCE

DAIRY FREE · GLUTEN FREE · NUT FREE · VEGAN

PREP TIME:
10 MINUTES,
PLUS 40 MINUTES
TO SOAK

COOK TIME:
4 HOURS

MAKES:
ABOUT 2 CUPS

FLAVOR NOTES
TANGY
SWEET
FRESH
WARM

TYPE OF SAUCE
CONDIMENT

While I was in Tunisia investigating spices and blends for Cooking with Spices, *I waltzed into the charming guesthouse Dar Souad in Tunis, armed with the understanding that* chermoula *is a spicy green sauce (as is the custom in Morocco and much of the Maghreb). The proprietor, Raja Maatar, explained that she would serve* chermoula *(also spelled charmoula) for breakfast. Raja kindly taught my cohorts and me that in Tunisia, it is reddish, sweet, and delicate. She was kind enough to lend me her recipe on the condition I come back to Tunisia and cook it with her.*

1¾ cups (½ pound) black raisins

1 quart water

Just under 1 cup extra-virgin olive oil, plus extra for drizzling

4 cups red onions (1 pound total), cut into strips

½ teaspoon ground cubeb pepper or freshly ground black pepper (see Ingredient tip)

2 teaspoons ground dried Damask rosebuds (see Ingredient tip)

½ teaspoon ground cloves

½ teaspoon ground cinnamon

½ teaspoon ground cayenne pepper

½ teaspoon sweet paprika

½ teaspoon ground turmeric

SPECIAL EQUIPMENT NEEDED

Blender, large cast iron pan or Dutch oven

1. Thoroughly wash the raisins several times to remove impurities, then drain and place in a large bowl. Pour in the water, and soak for 40 minutes. Transfer to a blender with the water, and blend to a mash. Push the raisin mash through a fine colander or sieve and mix to extract the juice.

2. In a large skillet over very low heat, heat the oil. Add the onions and cook for 2 hours, until they turn into a mash.

3. Pour the raisin mash in the pan. Stir in the cubeb, rosebuds, cloves, cinnamon, cayenne, paprika, and turmeric. Continue cooking for 2 more hours over low heat, until the sauce becomes thick.

4. Let cool and serve with a little more oil drizzled on top.

STORAGE: *1 month in a glass jar with a spoonful of olive oil on top to seal it*

INGREDIENT TIP: *Dried rosebuds can usually be found in teashops and specialty spice stores. If you can't find them at your local herbalist or apothecary, they are readily available online. Cubeb pepper can be ordered online and is easily replaced with black pepper, long pepper, or grains of paradise.*

PAIRINGS AND
SERVING IDEAS

MAINS

**White Fish Four
Ways (page 158)**

**Vegetable
Stir-Fry (page 169)**

**Pan-Seared Sea
Scallops (page 165)**

—

SIDES

**Bell Pepper Egg
Boats (page 172)**

**Pan-Roasted
Veggies (page 171)**

**Hand-Cut Zucchini
Noodles (page 174)**

Rice

Bread

Harissa Verte // SPICY GREEN HOT SAUCE

DAIRY FREE · GLUTEN FREE · NUT FREE · VEGAN

PREP TIME:
10 MINUTES

COOK TIME:
5 MINUTES

MAKES:
¾ CUP

FLAVOR NOTES
SPICY
BOTANICAL
PUNGENT
BITING

HEAT INDEX

TYPE OF SAUCE
CONDIMENT
SPREAD
MIX IN

Harissa is a popular condiment used all over North Africa and the Middle East. The most memorable harissa to ever hit my taste buds was in Tunisia. The kebab shop was open for prayer at roughly 3 a.m. and they slathered it on, hoping to catch my travel companions and me off guard with the spice level. Instead, it was paradise on my tongue. That was a red harissa, and my recreation of that spellbinder is in my previous book, Cooking with Spices. Green harissa is milder and less piquant than its more famous red cousin. As for the peppers, go with what's fresh. If your market has great-looking serrano peppers, pick those over soggy-looking jalapeños. I definitely recommend using whole spices for this recipe.

2 teaspoons coriander seeds

2 teaspoons cumin seeds

¼ cup extra-virgin olive oil, divided

4 jalapeño or green serrano chiles, stemmed and seeded

3 garlic cloves, peeled

1 small handful fresh parsley

1 small handful fresh mint leaves

1 tablespoon lemon juice

1 tablespoon apple cider vinegar

Salt

SPECIAL EQUIPMENT NEEDED

Spice grinder or mortar and pestle, food processor

1. In a small, dry pan over medium heat, toast the coriander and cumin seeds for 1 to 2 minutes to release their flavors. Let cool, and grind in a spice grinder or mortar and pestle.

2. In a medium skillet over medium heat, heat 1 tablespoon of oil. When hot, add the chiles and garlic and sauté for 3 to 5 minutes, until the edges brown.

3. Transfer to a food processor, and add the ground spices, parsley, mint, lemon juice, and vinegar. As the processor runs, drizzle in the remaining 3 tablespoons of oil.

4. Season with salt.

STORAGE: *2 weeks in the refrigerator in a glass jar or plastic container, or 6 months in the freezer in small plastic containers or frozen into cubes*

REPURPOSING TIP: *This can easily be made into red harissa by substituting reconstituted dried red chiles instead of the jalapeños. For more heat, leave in more of the stems, ribs, and seeds of the chile peppers. For less heat, remove them completely.*

PAIRINGS AND SERVING IDEAS

MAINS

Sautéed Thin-Cut Pork Chops (page 146)

Skirt Steak a la Parrilla (page 144)

Stovetop Lamb Loin Chops (page 147)

Baked Salmon (page 156)

Grilled White Fish (page 159)

Pan-Seared Sea Scallops (page 165)

Stovetop Mussels (page 162)

Vegetable Stir-Fry (page 169)

SIDES

Bell Pepper Egg Boats (page 172)

Pan-Roasted Veggies (page 171)

Mixed Green Salad (page 170)

Fluffy Couscous (page 181)

Bread

Toum // FLUFFY GARLIC SAUCE

DAIRY FREE • GLUTEN FREE • NUT FREE • VEGETARIAN

PREP TIME:
20 MINUTES

MAKES:
2 CUPS

FLAVOR NOTES
COOLING
FRESH
SAVORY

TYPE OF SAUCE
DIPPING
CONDIMENT
MARINADE

TJ Jawad Trad grew up sitting on the counter, watching his grandfather make this delicious Lebanese garlic sauce. Now he's the one who makes it for the entire family when they get together. It parallels the taste and texture of its relatives skordalia *in Greece,* tooma *in Egypt and* alioli *in Spain. Garlic is not as strong of an emulsifier as egg, for example in mayo, so following the steps to the letter is important if not using one. According to TJ, the perfect Toum has to be fluffy, potent, and white. Using vegetable oil instead of olive oil will help avoid making it yellowish. To make Toum that lasts longer, do not use egg whites (according to TJ's aunt). But note that without the egg it will be harder to emulsify.*

½ cup garlic cloves, peeled

1 teaspoon salt

1 egg white, divided

1½ cups vegetable oil, divided

¼ cup cold water, divided

¼ cup freshly squeezed lemon juice (from about 2 lemons)

SPECIAL EQUIPMENT NEEDED

Food processor

1. Remove any green parts or stems from the garlic cloves (they tend to be sour) by degerming them. Slice each clove in half lengthwise, then use your finger to take out the little stem in the middle of the garlic clove, as it's usually a bit sour, especially in old garlic.

2. In the food processor, process the garlic and salt for about 1 minute, until fine. Scrape down the sides for chunks, and process again.

3. With the food processor running, very slowly add half of the egg white. Then very slowly add ½ cup of oil. Very slowly add ⅛ cup of water.

4. With the processor still running, slowly add the remaining egg white, then another ½ cup of oil, then the remaining ⅛ cup of water. Very slowly add the remaining ½ cup of oil, and finally, the lemon juice. This emulsification process should take about 15 minutes.

STORAGE: *2 days in the refrigerator in a glass jar or plastic container, but best used immediately*

PAIRINGS AND SERVING IDEAS

MAINS

Stovetop Lamb Loin Chops (page 147)

Skirt Steak a la Parrilla (page 144)

Pan-Seared Boneless Chicken Thighs (page 149)

Kebabs

Shawarma

———

SIDES

Bell Pepper Egg Boats (page 172)

Pan-Roasted Veggies (page 171)

Potatoes Four Ways (page 175)

Zhoug // SPICY CILANTRO SAUCE

DAIRY FREE • GLUTEN FREE • NUT FREE • VEGAN

PREP TIME:
10 MINUTES

COOK TIME:
4 MINUTES

MAKES:
ABOUT 1 CUP

FLAVOR NOTES
ZESTY
HERBACEOUS
BOTANICAL
COOLING

HEAT INDEX

TYPE OF SAUCE
CONDIMENT
DIPPING

Chimichurri, pesto, harissa—Zhoug has been unfairly labeled the Yemeni version of each. It took on several name variations as it spread to Syria and Israel, such as zhug, sahawiq, and skhug. In all iterations, cilantro is the main component. It goes well on a variety of foods that the herbaceous quality of fresh herbs enhances. Fish, chicken, sandwiches, and pita are all instruments to carry the freshness of Zhoug to your senses. If, like me, you're one of those people for whom cilantro tastes like soap, perhaps you should skip to parsley-based Harissa Verte (page 92). Otherwise, dive in!

½ teaspoon cardamom pods

1 teaspoon cumin seeds

1 teaspoon caraway seeds (see Ingredient tip)

3 whole garlic cloves, peeled

½ cup plus 1 teaspoon extra-virgin olive oil, divided

1 cup packed fresh cilantro leaves (from about one big bunch), stemmed and chopped

3 jalapeño peppers or pepper of choice, chopped

½ teaspoon salt

1 squeeze fresh lemon juice

1 teaspoon white wine vinegar

1 teaspoon crushed red pepper flakes

SPECIAL EQUIPMENT NEEDED

Spice grinder or mortar and pestle, food processor

1. In a small, dry pan over medium heat, toast the cardamom, cumin, and caraway for 1 minute, then grind in the grinder or mortar and pestle.

2. In a small skillet over medium heat, roast the garlic in 1 teaspoon of oil until smoky and aromatic, 2 to 3 minutes.

3. In a food processor, combine the cardamom, cumin, caraway, garlic, cilantro, peppers, salt, lemon juice, vinegar, and red pepper flakes, and grind until you have a smooth paste.

STORAGE: *1 week in a glass jar or plastic container*

INGREDIENT TIP: *Caraway is full of volatile oils that break down when ground. Another reason to have a mortar and pestle on hand!*

REPURPOSING TIP: *Zhoug comes green, red, brown, and smoked. Mix and match chiles to achieve different results. Want a smoky red Zhoug? Use chipotle and ancho peppers and substitute smoked salt for regular salt.*

PAIRINGS AND
SERVING IDEAS

MAINS

Turkey Breast
Scaloppini Style
(page 148)

Pan-Seared
Boneless Chicken
Thighs (page 149)

Wild Salmon Four
Ways (page 155)

White Fish Four
Ways (page 158)

Pan-Seared Sea
Scallops (page 165)

Stovetop Mussels
(page 162)

Sautéed Shrimp
(page 164)

Tacos

SIDES

Pan-Roasted
Veggies (page 171)

Bell Pepper Egg
Boats (page 172)

Black Beans and
Wild Rice (page 186)

Fluffy Couscous
(page 181)

Quinoa and Lentils
(page 183)

Flatbread

Berbere Spiced Sauce //

SPICED WINE SAUCE

DAIRY FREE • GLUTEN FREE • NUT FREE

PREP TIME:
20 MINUTES,
PLUS 20 MINUTES
TO MARINATE

COOK TIME:
25 MINUTES

MAKES:
ABOUT 1 TO
1½ CUPS

FLAVOR NOTES

SPICY
MUSKY
HOT
WARM

HEAT INDEX

TYPE OF SAUCE

POUR OVER
COOK IN

Berbere is a cherished spice mix from Ethiopia that rouses the flavor in most stews and soups. Since the rub goes well on most foods, it is easily converted to a stew sauce by adding red wine and chicken or vegetable stock. Cook it down to a thicker sauce for stewed or seared lamb and steak. I always prefer to grind my own spices to maximize the flavor and freshness of the spice oils. This book is made for ease, so feel free to go with ground spices. Just know that toasting your spices whole and grinding them fresh will heighten the flavor significantly.

2 tablespoons freshly squeezed lime juice

½ onion, chopped

1 teaspoon salt

3 tablespoons vegetable oil, divided

½ teaspoon freshly ground cardamom

2 teaspoons freshly ground coriander

2 or 3 cloves, freshly ground

1 teaspoon freshly ground black pepper

¼ teaspoon freshly ground fenugreek

1 tablespoon hot paprika

½ teaspoon ground cayenne pepper

½ cup red wine

1 cinnamon stick

1 tablespoon tomato paste

½ cup chicken stock (page xv)

1. In a small bowl, combine the lime juice, onion, and salt, mix, and let stand for 20 minutes.

2. In a medium skillet over medium heat, heat 1 tablespoon of vegetable oil. Add the onion mixture and sauté it and any juices that have collected in the bowl until golden brown, 1 to 2 minutes.

3. In a small bowl, mix the cardamom, coriander, cloves, pepper, fenugreek, paprika, and cayenne together.

4. Turn the heat to medium-low, then add the spice mixture and the remaining 2 tablespoons of oil to the pan. Stir to coat the onions evenly.

5. Immediately add the wine, cinnamon stick, and tomato paste, and stir. When mixed thoroughly, simmer for 5 minutes. Then add the stock.

6. For a thinner sauce for fish and lentils, simmer for about 10 minutes. For a thicker sauce for poultry and meats, simmer for about 20 minutes. Remove the cinnamon stick and serve.

STORAGE: *1 to 2 weeks in the refrigerator in a glass jar or plastic container*

INGREDIENT TIP: *This recipe easily converts to vegan—simply use a vegetable stock instead of chicken stock.*

REPURPOSING TIP: *Use thin berbere sauce as a marinade. Marinate overnight for heavier meats, a couple of hours for poultry.*

PAIRINGS AND
SERVING IDEAS

MAINS

Grilled
Flanken-Style
Ribs (page 143)

Stovetop Lamb Loin
Chops (page 147)

Skirt Steak a la
Parrilla (page 144)

Pan-Seared
Boneless Chicken
Thighs (page 149)

White Fish Four
Ways (page 158)

SIDES

Potatoes Four
Ways (page 175)

Quinoa and Lentils
(page 183)

Black Beans and
Wild Rice (page 186)

Tomato "Simba Kali" Sauce //

"FIERCE" TOMATO SAUCE

DAIRY FREE • GLUTEN FREE • NUT FREE

PREP TIME:
10 MINUTES

COOK TIME:
1 HOUR

MAKES:
ABOUT 3 TO
4 CUPS

FLAVOR NOTES
SPICY
WARM
BITING

HEAT INDEX

TYPE OF SAUCE
POUR OVER
COOK IN

This recipe comes from Jack Hatzfeld and James Kihara Munuhe. James is from Nairobi and grew up teaching his cousin Jack songs and phrases in Swahili. When it came time to name this sauce, which according to the pair "embodies the flavors and spices used in Kenya," they went with Simba Kali, which means "fierce lion." The sauce itself is a variation on a widely used tomato sauce, intended to be used with almost anything except fish, which can't as easily stand up to its flavor. If you prefer using fresh tomatoes, use roughly 6 to 8 Roma tomatoes or any sweet, firm-when-peeled equivalent.

1½ teaspoon extra-virgin olive oil

1 (35-ounce) can peeled tomatoes, such as San Marzano

½ teaspoon ground nutmeg

¼ teaspoon ground cloves

1½ tablespoons crushed red pepper flakes

½ teaspoon ground cardamom

2 dried bay leaves

1 cinnamon stick

½ teaspoon ground allspice

½ cup beef stock (page xv)

2 tablespoons chopped fresh cilantro

Juice of ½ lemon

Salt

1. In a medium skillet over medium heat, heat the olive oil for 1 minute. Pour in the tomatoes with their juices and cook, mixing, for 2 to 3 minutes. When soft, break up the tomatoes with a wooden spoon or mixing utensil.

2. Add the nutmeg, cloves, red pepper flakes, cardamom, bay leaves, cinnamon stick, allspice, stock, cilantro, and lemon juice, season with salt, and stir. Turn the heat to low.

3. Simmer uncovered for 1 hour, mixing every so often.

4. Remove the cinnamon and bay leaves, if you prefer, and serve.

STORAGE: *1 to 2 weeks in the refrigerator in a glass jar or plastic container, or months in the freezer in a plastic container; you can also vacuum seal this sauce in jars using a canning process, and it will keep for a year or more*

PAIRINGS AND
SERVING IDEAS

MAINS

Grilled
Flanken-Style
Ribs (page 143)

Sautéed
Thin-Cut Pork
Chops (page 146)

Stovetop Lamb Loin
Chops (page 147)

Skirt Steak a la
Parrilla (page 144)

Pan-Seared
Boneless Chicken
Thighs (page 149)

Stovetop Mussels
(page 162)

SIDES

Hand-Cut Zucchini
Noodles (page 174)

Fluffy Couscous
(page 181)

Quinoa and Lentils
(page 183)

Homemade Pasta
Noodles (page 184)

Black Beans and
Wild Rice (page 186)

Monkey Gland Sauce //

TANGY BARBECUE SAUCE

DAIRY FREE • NUT FREE

PREP TIME:
5 MINUTES

COOK TIME:
40 MINUTES

MAKES:
2½ CUPS

FLAVOR NOTES

TANGY

SWEET

MUSKY

HEAT INDEX

TYPE OF SAUCE

CONDIMENT

POUR OVER

COOK IN

DIPPING

*T*here are no primate parts in this sauce. Legend has it that the sauce was developed at the storied but troubled Carlton Hotel in Johannesburg when the French chefs threw what they had available into a big pot: ketchup, Worcestershire sauce, and mustard. The sauce was a hit, but what about the name? Another piece of sauce lore suggests Dr. Serge Voronoff—a Russian doctor who was experimenting with monkey sex glands and human male virility—frequented the Savoy Hotel in London, where a version of the sauce was served. Some Monkey Gland Sauce recipes call for ketchup, but mine, which was constructed with counsel from Yolandé van Heerden, is more vinegary than the kind they use in South Africa.

1 tablespoon vegetable oil or grapeseed oil

1 to 2 shallots, minced

3 garlic cloves, minced

1 (14-ounce) can peeled tomatoes, chopped

¼ cup tomato paste

¾ cup chutney (see Ingredient tip)

1 to 2 tablespoons brown sugar

2 tablespoons balsamic vinegar

3 tablespoons Worcestershire sauce

½ cup chicken stock (page xv)

1 tablespoon Tabasco sauce

Salt

Freshly ground black pepper

1. In a medium skillet or saucepan over medium heat, heat the oil. Add the shallots and garlic, and cook until translucent, about 2 minutes. Add the tomatoes and tomato paste, and stir. When sizzling, add the chutney, sugar, vinegar, and Worcestershire sauce. Stir.

2. Turn the heat to low. Add the chicken stock, stir, and simmer uncovered for 30 to 35 minutes, until a thick sauce develops. Add the Tabasco sauce, and season with salt and pepper.

STORAGE: *2 weeks in the refrigerator in a glass jar or plastic container, or freeze in ice cube trays and keep 3 months in the freezer in freezer bags*

INGREDIENT TIP: *No monkey glands needed! But chutney certainly is a requirement. The classic brand to use is Mrs. Ball's—which can be bought in many flavors online. However, I like to use Mango Chutney (page 12) as a freshly made stand-in.*

PAIRINGS AND
SERVING IDEAS

MAINS

Skirt Steak a la Parrilla (page 144)

Grilled Flanken-Style Ribs (page 143)

Sautéed Thin-Cut Pork Chops (page 146)

Stovetop Lamb Loin Chops (page 147)

Turkey Breast Scaloppini Style (page 148)

Pan-Seared Boneless Chicken Thighs (page 149)

Pan-Seared Crispy-Skin Duck Breast (page 150)

SIDES

Potatoes Four Ways (page 175)

Black Beans and Wild Rice (page 186)

4

EUROPE

EUROPE IS HOME TO THE CLASSIC FRENCH SAUCES, but for a world sauces cookbook, the endeavor is to search beyond. As a New Orleans resident, I'm a card-carrying member of the roux fan club. So while I'm compelled to nod to those matriarch sauces and their children, in this chapter I want to purposefully steer you away from those heavy and thick French sauces and down the rabbit hole into the world of lesser known—and non-exhaustively covered—regions and sauces.

I retain from my grandmother, Nonna Yvelise, her Italian citizenship and passion for feeding people ragù (page 108). It is also a certainty in my family that although many have tried, Zia Elda, my great aunt, makes the pesto. Every time I go home to Chiavari, in the Italian Riviera, I plead with her to make it so I can again see the perfect consistency firsthand. My own has come a long way over the years.

These regional sauces—from a very specific place, and often a very specific family—will bring you to an exact place and story. Rødgrød (page 130), I hope, transports you to the childhood garden home of Ole Storm Hansen, who shared it. Marti Buckley contributed Salsa Vizcaína (page 114), which will teleport your senses directly to Basque Country where I met her over *pintxos*. Her lens into Basque gastronomy and cuisine, through her blog *Blank Palate*, is unrivaled.

Like many of the sauces in this book, the recipe for the delightful Ajika (page 136) comes from the kind of European mother who will make a giant batch and freeze it for the winter months in vacuum-sealed jars. While it has stood the test of time, I had to cut it by two-thirds so you don't have to buy 5½ pounds of zucchini (but by all means, do so if you can—a canned jar of Ajika is a great gift).

It would be dubious to trust any sauce book without a mustard sauce (Senfsauce [page 128] here) and a horseradish sauce (Pepparrotsås [page 134]—in Nordic languages horseradish is translated as "pepper-root"). And, as in Wonderland when Alice ponders whether to consume a cake on top of which EAT ME is spelled out in currants, the lingonberries or cranberries in Sweden's Lingonsås (page 132) might call you to do the same.

Ragù della Nonna //

NONNA'S TOMATO SAUCE

GLUTEN FREE • NUT FREE

PREP TIME:
20 MINUTES

COOK TIME:
1½ HOURS

MAKES:
ABOUT 4 CUPS

FLAVOR NOTES
SAVORY
WARM
FULL
BRIGHT

TYPE OF SAUCE
POUR OVER
COOK IN

Several summers ago I went to Chiavari, Italy, to learn the family recipes from my Nonna. As a child, ravioli in ragù was one of the only foods I would voluntarily consume. Though Bolognese is the arguably most classic of Italian tomato pasta sauces, I have been raised to prefer this recipe—which admittedly takes some unholy liberties with the official version. But what tastes better than nostalgia? If you're keen to know what made little Markino (as Nonna calls me) finally eat, this sauce is for you. I've added ground beef and two kinds of sausage here, but this ragù can be made with anything from veggies to llama meat (mother approved), or without a protein for a vegetarian tomato sauce.

- 2 tablespoons extra-virgin olive oil, divided, plus more as needed
- 2 garlic cloves, minced, divided
- 1 carrot, peeled and minced
- ½ onion, minced
- 1 celery stalk, minced
- 2 dried bay leaves
- 1 fresh rosemary sprig
- 2 tablespoons herbes de Provence
- ⅓ pound ground beef
- ⅓ pound Italian sausage meat
- ⅓ pound spicy Italian sausage meat
- ½ cup white wine
- ½ cup chicken or vegetable stock (page xv)
- 1 handful pine nuts
- Freshly ground black pepper
- 2 cups Simple Tomato Sauce (page xiv)
- 2 tablespoons tomato paste
- ½ cup grated Parmigiano-Reggiano cheese
- Salt

1. In a large, heavy sauté pan or Dutch oven over medium-high heat, combine 1 tablespoon of olive oil, 1 minced garlic clove, and the carrot, onion, celery, bay leaves, rosemary sprig, and herbes de Provence. Cook until the garlic begins to brown, about 5 minutes.

2. Return the pan to medium-high heat. Heat the remaining 1 tablespoon of olive oil. Add the ground beef and sausage (or other protein) to the pan and brown until cooked through, about 5 minutes. Add a little more olive oil as needed. Pour in the wine and stock. Add the pine nuts, and season with pepper.

3. Pour the tomato sauce and paste into the pan with the meat, and mix. Reduce the heat to low, cover, and let simmer, occasionally adding the cheese in handfuls and stirring until all is incorporated. The sauce should be thick and hearty but should also coat pasta evenly without being too chunky. This can take an hour or up to an hour and a half, but watch the sauce and stir occasionally so it doesn't burn on the bottom of the pan. Season with salt.

STORAGE: *2 weeks in the refrigerator in a glass jar or plastic container or months in the freezer in plastic containers*

REPURPOSING TIP: *If you're making a regular tomato sauce without meat, just leave it out and keep going with the recipe. Alternatively, substitute ground turkey or chicken, tofu or tempeh, or add some pan-seared vegetables. If you don't have a can of tomatoes for the Simple Tomato Sauce (page xiv), equal parts tomato paste and water with a pinch of salt and sugar will suffice.*

PAIRINGS AND
SERVING IDEAS

MAINS

**Turkey Breast
Scaloppini Style
(page 148)**

**Pan-Seared
Boneless Chicken
Thighs (page 149)**

**Homemade Pasta
Noodles (page 184)**

**Hand-Rolled
Gnocchi (page 187)**

**Hand-Cut Zucchini
Noodles (page 174)**

Pizza

Lasagna

SIDES

**Potatoes Four
Ways (page 175)**

Bread

Pesto della Zia // ZIA ELDA'S PESTO LIGURE

GLUTEN FREE • NUT FREE • VEGETARIAN

PREP TIME:
30 MINUTES
——
MAKES:
ABOUT 1 TO
2 CUPS

FLAVOR NOTES
FLORAL
HERBACEOUS
COOLING
BUTTERY

TYPE OF SAUCE
CONDIMENT
POUR OVER

Liguria, on the northwestern coast of Italy where my mother, Cristina, was born, is where pesto originated. Pesto, in its truest form, is made with basil and olive oil. In my unsolicited opinion, all others should be defined by type—arugula pesto, kale pesto, and so on—but never say "basil pesto." That's just pesto. My Italian mother, grandmother, great aunt, and I have a running competition for who makes the best pesto. Of course, Zia Elda—my masterful great aunt—always makes it the best because she has a feel for putting in just *the right amount of garlic* (she says Americans tend to overdose, a theme in my family you'll notice). She has nearly a century of experience, after all. This is how she does it.

4 generous handfuls fresh basil leaves, divided

1 cup extra-virgin olive oil, divided

¾ cup (about 3 ounces) grated Parmigiano-Reggiano cheese (see Ingredient tip)

1 tablespoon pine nuts

1 or 2 garlic cloves, chopped

SPECIAL EQUIPMENT NEEDED

Food processor

1. In a small saucepan of boiling water, very quickly blanch all the basil for 5 seconds to prevent darkening (my mom's trick). Strain.

2. In the bowl of the food processor, combine about three-quarters of the basil with ¾ cup of olive oil, and process. Add 8 tablespoons of cheese while the food processor runs. Pulse the food processor, and add the pine nuts and garlic. (If you like it more garlicky, despite what Zia says, go ahead and add a bit more.)

3. Dip a spoon in to taste. The consistency will depend on the size of the basil leaves and the oil you used. Balance and texture is the key. With the remaining ¼ cup of oil, ¼ cup of cheese, and basil, add small portions of each, as follows: If the pesto doesn't drip off the spoon, then add a bit of oil until it is less thick. If it falls too readily—in a stream—then add basil and cheese. You shouldn't taste the cheese as the first, most forward flavor, so add more oil and basil if you do.

STORAGE: *1 week in the refrigerator in a glass jar or plastic container, or 6 months in the freezer; use small plastic containers and freeze in portion sizes*

INGREDIENT TIP: *Not all Parmesan cheese is Parmesan cheese. Italian cheese producers were successful in getting Parmigiano DOC status, which is certification of origin and production standards and a protection against fakes. However, in the United States, such protection is given only for the word Parmigiano—meaning that "Parmesan cheese" will likely not be Parmigiano. Do yourself and your taste buds a favor and buy Parmigiano-Reggiano (you'll see it imprinted on the rind).*

PAIRINGS AND
SERVING IDEAS

MAINS

**Pan-Seared
Boneless Chicken
Thighs (page 149)**

**Wild Salmon Four
Ways (page 155)**

**White Fish Four
Ways (page 158)**

**Pan-Seared Sea
Scallops (page 165)**

**Stovetop Mussels
(page 162)**

**Sautéed Shrimp
(page 164)**

**Hand-Cut Zucchini
Noodles (page 174)**

**Hand-Rolled
Gnocchi (page 187)**

**Homemade Pasta
Noodles (page 184)**

SIDES

**Smashed Garlic Red
Potatoes (page 176)**

**Roasted Fingerling
Potatoes (page 177)**

Bread

Romesco // ROASTED RED PEPPER SAUCE

DAIRY FREE • VEGAN

PREP TIME:
15 MINUTES,
PLUS 30 MINUTES
TO BLEND

COOK TIME:
25 MINUTES

MAKES:
ABOUT 1⅔ CUPS

FLAVOR NOTES
ZESTY
PUNGENT
SWEET
FRESH

TYPE OF SAUCE
CONDIMENT
DIPPING
COOK IN

Romesco is a Catalan sauce originally made by fishermen in the region to accompany the catch. There are definitive regional Catalan variations: salvitxada (thinner, vinegar-based, and poured on a variety of charred green onions called calçots) and xató (an endive and salted cod salad generally served with romesco). Romesco, however, has transformed from using reconstituted ñora peppers and blanched almonds to sauces with all manner of capsicums and hazelnuts or walnuts. Vince Mancini provided his version, which nods to salvitxada by incorporating charred scallion into the sauce itself.

1 red bell pepper

1 ripe, golf-ball-size tomato

1 large scallion, trimmed and cleaned

3 or 4 whole garlic cloves, unpeeled

2 teaspoons smoked Spanish pimentón (paprika)

2 medallion-size (½-inch) French baguette slices

2 tablespoons sherry vinegar

1 teaspoon salt

3 heaping tablespoons Marcona almonds or slivered almonds

About ⅓ cup extra-virgin olive oil, as needed

SPECIAL EQUIPMENT NEEDED

Food processor, broiler or gas range/grill

1. Set an oven rack to the middle, and preheat your broiler to high.

2. In a small broiler pan, place the red bell pepper, tomato, scallion, and garlic. Broil on high, turning every 5 minutes, for about 10 minutes for the onion, 15 minutes for the tomato

and garlic, and 25 minutes for the pepper, until the pepper is "leoparded" (as much black char as red on the skin). Or char the skins over the flame on your gas range, using a pair of tongs. The skin of the tomato should blacken and split, becoming easy to peel off. The garlic should get soft enough that you can squish it between your fingers. The scallion should have a good char, too.

3. Let everything cool, then peel the skins off the pepper, garlic, and tomato. Seed and stem the pepper.

4. In the food processor, combine the cooked vegetables, paprika, baguette, vinegar, and salt, and pulse into a purée. Add the almonds, and pulse. Then add the olive oil while the processor is running, and process until smooth but chunky. It should appear like chunky mashed potatoes but stir thinner, like pesto.

5. Transfer to a bowl and let cool for 20 to 30 minutes so the flavors can blend.

STORAGE: *1 to 2 weeks in the refrigerator in a glass jar or plastic container, or 6 weeks in the freezer in plastic containers*

REPURPOSING TIP: *Add a spoonful or two to your soup, risotto, or paella.*

PAIRINGS AND
SERVING IDEAS

MAINS

Sautéed
Thin-Cut Pork
Chops (page 146)

Stovetop Lamb Loin
Chops (page 147)

Skirt Steak a la
Parrilla (page 144)

Wild Salmon Four
Ways (page 155)

White Fish Four
Ways (page 158)

Pan-Seared Sea
Scallops (page 165)

Stovetop Mussels
(page 162)

Sautéed Shrimp
(page 164)

SIDES

Pan-Roasted
Veggies (page 171)

Hand-Cut Zucchini
Noodles (page 174)

Roasted Fingerling
Potatoes (page 177)

Hand-Rolled
Gnocchi (page 187)

Quinoa and Lentils
(page 183)

Homemade Pasta
Noodles (page 184)

Salsa Vizcaína // BISCAYNE SAUCE

DAIRY FREE • GLUTEN FREE • NUT FREE

PREP TIME:
10 MINUTES,
PLUS 1 HOUR TO
SOAK

COOK TIME:
25 MINUTES

MAKES:
ABOUT 1½ TO
2½ CUPS

FLAVOR NOTES
WARM
PIQUANT
AROMATIC

HEAT INDEX
🌶🌶🌶🌶🌶

TYPE OF SAUCE
POUR OVER
COOK IN
BASE

One of the Basque Country's most beloved sauces, *Salsa Vizcaína* is also one of its most versatile. *Bizkaia, its namesake province, is on the coast, so this sauce is often made with salted cod in the dish* Bakailaoa Bizkaiko Erara. *It appears in a similar form with salted cod in Marti Buckley's iconic cookbook* Basque Country, *though there are as many versions as Basque home cooks. Some incorporate ham, others throw in shellfish, so feel free to tinker as you see fit. This sauce also makes a great base for a red pasta sauce or a minestrone-type vegetable soup. Marti notes that Basque cooks will use flour or a piece of bread to solidify or thicken the sauce.*

12 dried choricero peppers (or 6 tablespoons jarred choricero pulp; see Ingredient tip)

3 to 4 cups warm water

⅔ cup extra-virgin olive oil

2 garlic cloves, sliced

3 red onions, minced

1 fresh parsley sprig

1½ cups fish, chicken, or vegetable stock (page xv)

½ cup Simple Tomato Sauce (page xiv)

SPECIAL EQUIPMENT NEEDED

Food mill

1. In a small bowl, reconstitute the peppers in the warm water for up to an hour. Drain and dry. Stem and seed the peppers, scrape the pulp from the skin with a knife, and discard the skin. Set the choricero pulp aside.

2. In a medium saucepan over medium heat, heat the olive oil. Add the garlic. When the garlic starts to "dance" and turns golden, remove from the oil and discard. Add the onions and parsley to the pan, and cook until the onions are golden and softened, about 5 minutes. Remove the pan from the heat, and drain any excess oil. Add the pepper pulp, and return the pan to medium-high heat for about 30 seconds. Add the stock and tomato sauce. Cook for 5 minutes, until the sauce is mixed and slightly thickened.

3. Pour the sauce into a food mill and press through with a bit of force using a ladle or wooden spoon. Discard the solids.

4. Return the liquid sauce to the saucepan and heat for 5 to 10 minutes, until nice and thick.

5. If you're using this sauce for fish, ham, meatballs, or another protein, finish them by cooking them in the sauce for their final minutes to warm them through and absorb the flavors.

STORAGE: *1 to 2 weeks in the refrigerator in a glass jar or plastic container, but best used within a day or two*

INGREDIENT TIP: *Choricero peppers are Basque chiles that are hung outside to dry and have a sweet, spicy flavor. Find them or their jarred pulp online.*

PAIRINGS AND
SERVING IDEAS

MAINS

Sautéed
Thin-Cut Pork
Chops (page 146)

Stovetop Lamb Loin
Chops (page 147)

Grilled White
Fish (page 159)

Grilled Salmon
(page 156)

Sautéed Shrimp
(page 164)

Pan-Seared Sea
Scallops (page 165)

Stovetop Mussels
(page 162)

Grilled ham

SIDES

Duck Fat Fries
(page 176)

Bread

Sauce Forestière // MUSHROOM CREAM SAUCE

GLUTEN FREE • NUT FREE • VEGETARIAN

PREP TIME:
10 MINUTES

COOK TIME:
25 MINUTES

MAKES:
²/₃ TO 1⅓ CUPS

FLAVOR NOTES
CREAMY
BUTTERY
UMAMI
WARM

TYPE OF SAUCE
POUR OVER

*S*auce forestière *means sauce "of the forest," and generally refers to wild mushrooms in cream over* a base of poultry, beef, or fish that can be paired with pasta or potatoes. For this recipe, I went to Travis Nicks, who uses more mushrooms in cooking than anyone I know. What makes Travis such a fun guy is his particularity *when it comes to cooking with mushrooms. He recommends king oyster mushrooms for this sauce, or fresh shiitake or porcini as a distant second and third.*

2 tablespoons unsalted butter

½ pound king oyster, shiitake, or porcini mushrooms, diced small

1 shallot, chopped

1 (½-inch) piece fresh ginger, minced

¼ cup dry white wine or rosé

½ cup heavy (whipping) cream

Splash port or madeira wine (optional)

1 teaspoon fresh thyme leaves

1 teaspoon chopped fresh parsley

Salt

Freshly ground black pepper

SPECIAL EQUIPMENT NEEDED

Food processor

1. In a medium skillet over low heat, melt the butter until the foam dissipates. Add the mushrooms, and sauté for 5 minutes, until softened and golden. Add the shallot and ginger, and cook until browned, 2 to 5 minutes more.

2. In a separate small saucepan, quickly boil the wine for 1 minute to remove any harshness. Add the heavy cream, wine, and port (if using), and mix. Bring just to a soft boil, and take the pan off the heat.

3. Let the mushrooms infuse in the cream for 5 minutes. In a food processor, process the mushroom-cream mixture until the sauce is quite smooth. For an alternate version, strain out the solids and serve as a mushroom-infused cream sauce.

4. Stir in the thyme and parsley, and season with salt and pepper.

STORAGE: *Best used immediately*

PAIRINGS AND
SERVING IDEAS

MAINS

Skirt Steak a la
Parrilla (page 144)

Sautéed
Thin-Cut Pork
Chops (page 146)

Stovetop Lamb Loin
Chops (page 147)

Turkey Breast
Scaloppini Style
(page 148)

Pan-Seared
Boneless Chicken
Thighs (page 149)

Grilled Salmon
(page 156)

Hand-Rolled
Gnocchi (page 187)

Homemade Pasta
Noodles (page 184)

SIDES

Smashed Garlic Red
Potatoes (page 176)

Roasted Fingerling
Potatoes (page 177)

Pan-Roasted
Veggies (page 171)

Piri Piri Whiskey Sauce // HOT SAUCE

DAIRY FREE • GLUTEN FREE • NUT FREE • VEGETARIAN (SAUCE TWO IS VEGAN)

PREP TIME:
5 MINUTES,
PLUS 1 HOUR
TO REST FOR
SAUCE ONE,
2 WEEKS TO REST
FOR SAUCE TWO

MAKES:
ABOUT 2 TO
3 CUPS

FLAVOR NOTES

SPICY
OAKY
WOODY
BITING

HEAT INDEX

TYPE OF SAUCE

POUR OVER
COOK IN
MIX IN
BASE

As part of the exchange that accompanied Portuguese exploration and colonization, chile peppers—piri piri ones specifically—came to Lisbon (allegedly by way of their colony in Mozambique) when that city was still at the very center of the trading universe. In Barcelona in 2005, I was detoured to Portugal by a troupe of Portuguese architecture students and introduced, through staying at their houses and meeting their parents, to the culinary delights of Iberia's western edge. My friend Manuel Banazol sent me his grandfather's recipe, which can be made two ways and put on anything for a burst of heat. Mix either with mayo or tahini for a ridiculously delicious sandwich spread.

SAUCE ONE

5 or 6 fresh chiles, such as cayenne or serrano, stemmed but with seeds included

1 or 2 whole garlic cloves, peeled

1 small shallot, peeled

1½ ounces whiskey

1½ ounces extra-virgin olive oil

1 tablespoon vinegar

Pinch salt

1 tablespoon honey

1 teaspoon balsamic vinegar

SPECIAL EQUIPMENT NEEDED

Blender

1. In a blender, combine the chiles, garlic, shallot, whiskey, olive oil, vinegar, salt, honey, and balsamic. Transfer to a medium bowl.

2. Let sit for an hour, then mix again with a spoon.

SAUCE TWO

½ cup whole dried chiles (roughly 125–150 dried piri piri chiles or 20–25 dried cayenne or serrano chiles)

1 cup whiskey

1 cup extra-virgin olive oil

1 or 2 whole garlic cloves, peeled

1 dried bay leaf

1. In a glass bottle or mason jar with a lid, combine the chiles and whiskey and shake once a day for a week.

2. Add the olive oil, garlic, and bay leaf, and leave the mixture for another week.

3. Pour over any meal for a blast of heat.

STORAGE: *Sauce One keeps for 3 to 4 weeks in the refrigerator in a glass jar; Sauce Two will last a year in a mason jar*

PAIRINGS AND
SERVING IDEAS

MAINS

Sautéed
Thin-Cut Pork
Chops (page 146)

Grilled
Flanken-Style
Ribs (page 143)

Sautéed Shrimp
(page 164)

Pan-Seared Sea
Scallops (page 165)

Stovetop Mussels
(page 162)

White Fish Four
Ways (page 158)

Vegetable
Stir-Fry (page 169)

SIDES

Bell Pepper Egg
Boats (page 172)

Potatoes Four
Ways (page 175)

Black Beans and
Wild Rice (page 186)

Quinoa and Lentils
(page 183)

Fondue à la Bière // ALPINE CHEESE SAUCE

NUT FREE • VEGETARIAN

PREP TIME:
10 MINUTES

COOK TIME:
15 MINUTES

MAKES:
2½ CUPS

FLAVOR NOTES
CREAMY
WARM
BUTTERY
VELVETY

TYPE OF SAUCE
DIPPING
POUR OVER

Melted cheese and wine has been a part of Swiss fare since at least the seventeenth century, but it exploded into world consciousness because of the marketing efforts of the Swiss Cheese Union (yes, that's a thing) and international fascination with Heidi, the Swiss kids' book. Fondue etymologically derives from the French verb fondre, "to melt." Liberties with the sauce have accommodated chocolate and fruit compotes, or even just oil and fat for steak. For this version, use deliciously dark beer like Chimay, or conjure the Alps with an Alpine beer like Zermatt Bier. Use whichever cheeses you like, but Alpine and soft cheeses work best. Besides those listed, consider Comté, Gouda, or Cheddar. Leave extra beer and cheese to the side so you can perfect your mixture.

1 tablespoon extra-virgin olive oil

½ cup shallots, diced

2 fresh rosemary sprigs

1 whole garlic clove, peeled

1⅓ cups grated Gruyère cheese

1 cup grated Emmental cheese

1⅓ cups grated vacherin or fontina cheese

4½ teaspoons cornstarch

1 cup plus 1 tablespoon brown beer, such as Chimay

Juice of 1 lemon

1 tablespoon vin santo or any fortified wine, such as port

Salt

Freshly ground black pepper

Freshly grated nutmeg

1. In a large, heavy-bottomed pan, fondue pot, or cast iron skillet over medium heat, heat the oil. Add the shallots, rosemary, and garlic clove, and sauté until the shallots turn golden and caramelize, 5 to 7 minutes. Transfer everything to a small dish. Strip the rosemary, and discard the stems.

2. Smash the garlic clove, and rub the interior of the skillet with it, covering the bottom and about an inch up on all sides. Discard the garlic.

3. In a large bowl, mix the cheeses together. Add the cornstarch, mix, and set aside.

4. In the skillet over medium heat, combine the beer and lemon juice and bring to a soft boil. Reduce the heat to low, and add a handful of the cheese mixture to the skillet. Stir constantly in small circles or figure eights, and as the cheese melts, add another handful. Continue until all the cheese is melted.

5. The mixture should be nice and thick, like the consistency of a hollandaise or ketchup, so it will stick to bread. This may require a little finesse. If it's too thin, and the cheese just runs off what you dip into it, add small handfuls of cheese until it thickens. If the cheese is very clumpy and thick, add a splash of beer.

6. Add the vin santo, and mix. Return to a simmer for 1 minute or so. Mix in the shallots and rosemary. Season with salt and pepper. Grate some nutmeg over the dish, and serve.

STORAGE: *2 days in the refrigerator in a glass jar or plastic container, but best used immediately*

REPURPOSING TIP: *For the best macaroni and cheese of your life, reheat leftover fondue in a saucepan over low heat with a healthy dollop of heavy (whipping) cream. Use about a 2-to-1 ratio of fondue to cream, but if you're unsure, just add a little cream, stir, add some more, and continue until the sauce is silky.*

PAIRINGS AND SERVING IDEAS

MAINS

Sautéed
Thin-Cut Pork
Chops (page 146)

Turkey Breast
Scaloppini Style
(page 148)

Hand-Rolled
Gnocchi (page 187)

Homemade Pasta
Noodles (page 184)

Sausages

Burgers

Meatballs

SIDES

Bell Pepper Egg
Boats (page 172)

Pan-Roasted
Veggies (page 171)

Potatoes Four
Ways (page 175)

Sliced fruit

Bread

Apple Gastrique // APPLESAUCE

GLUTEN FREE • NUT FREE • VEGETARIAN

PREP TIME:
10 MINUTES,
PLUS 10 MINUTES
TO REST

COOK TIME:
20 MINUTES

MAKES:
ABOUT 3 TO
4 CUPS

FLAVOR NOTES
SWEET
TANGY
WARM
EARTHY

TYPE OF SAUCE
CONDIMENT
POUR OVER
SPREAD

The origins of applesauce are murky. Here I've attributed it to England because of its inclusion in several eighteenth century English cookbooks, which apparently are the first mentions of the dish. In the 1739 edition of Compleat Housewife, it accompanied duck but has since gone on to become wildly popular with all types of game and pork. This recipe is intended to be savory, not applesauce as a dessert. However, as an offshoot of my mom's applesauce recipe, it can be eaten right out of the jar. Use tart apples like Granny Smith and/or McIntosh, or a combination.

4 to 6 apples

Salt

1 cup unfiltered apple cider vinegar

2 tablespoons unsalted butter

1 cup brown sugar

1 teaspoon ground cinnamon

1 teaspoon ground nutmeg

1 teaspoon grated fresh ginger

Fresh thyme leaves, for seasoning

Ground cayenne pepper, for seasoning

Freshly ground allspice, for seasoning

SPECIAL EQUIPMENT NEEDED

Chinois or metal strainer, food processor

1. Peel, core, and cube the apples, and set aside.

2. In a medium bowl, combine the apple peels, a pinch of salt, and the vinegar. Set aside.

3. In a medium saucepan over medium heat, melt the butter. Add the apple cubes, and sauté for 5 minutes. Add the sugar, and raise the heat to high. Stir often, being attentive so nothing chars. When the apples start to caramelize, strain the vinegar mixture into the apple caramel and discard the peels. Let boil for about 1 minute, and reduce the heat to low.

4. Simmer to reduce the entire mixture for about 15 minutes, until the apples are soft and the desired thickness is achieved. Add the cinnamon, nutmeg, and ginger, and season as you like with thyme, cayenne, and allspice.

5. Remove from the heat. Let sit for 5 to 10 minutes, then drain, saving the liquid. Transfer the apples to the food processor, and give a couple of pulses until a mash consistency develops. Add the liquid back in as you pulse. It should eventually have small chunks of apple hidden among the smoothness of the sauce.

6. Season with salt, then can or refrigerate.

STORAGE: *1 to 2 weeks in the refrigerator in a glass jar or plastic container, or can this sauce in mason jars to keep for a long time*

REPURPOSING TIP: *You can make apple butter by cooking down applesauce in a saucepan until it becomes smooth and thick.*

PAIRINGS AND
SERVING IDEAS

MAINS

Sautéed
Thin-Cut Pork
Chops (page 146)

Pan-Seared
Crispy-Skin Duck
Breast (page 150)

Turkey Breast
Scaloppini Style
(page 148)

Pan-Seared
Boneless Chicken
Thighs (page 149)

SIDES

Potatoes Four
Ways (page 175)

Quinoa and Lentils
(page 183)

Sauce Liégeoise //

SWEET AND SAVORY BROWN SAUCE

NUT FREE

PREP TIME:
10 MINUTES

COOK TIME:
1 HOUR
40 MINUTES

MAKES:
ABOUT 1½ TO
2 CUPS

FLAVOR NOTES
NUTTY
SWEET
RESONANT
UMAMI

TYPE OF SAUCE
POUR OVER
COOK IN
DIPPING

I learned about this sauce from my neighbor Camille De Gend, who hails from the Belgian city of Liège. *This sauce gets an abundance of flavor from a glaze called* sirop de Liège, *which is made by boiling down apple and pear juices into a syrup. The sauce is used to cook* boulets à la liégeoise *(meatballs in Liège sauce, traditionally served with fries and mayonnaise) but can be used for all sorts of gamey meats and poultry, like rabbit, boar, or turkey. Some places in Belgium give you the option to top your fries with sauce Liégeoise, but those of us who like our fries crispy love having it on the side for dipping, especially with mayonnaise. Since 1996 there has been a competition to award a Crystal Meatball (Le Boulet de Cristal) to the best maker of the dish.*

1 tablespoon vegetable oil

1 tablespoon butter

1 large onion, chopped

1 garlic clove, crushed

5 teaspoons sirop de Liège, divided (see Ingredient tip)

1 tablespoon red wine vinegar

1 tablespoon flour

1½ cups chicken, veal, or vegetable stock (page xv)

1½ cups brown beer (not too bitter)

2 cloves

1 bunch fresh thyme

2 dried bay leaves

1 tablespoon mustard

1 small handful currants

Salt

Freshly ground black pepper

SPECIAL EQUIPMENT NEEDED

Cast iron skillet or Dutch oven

1. In a large cast iron skillet or Dutch oven over medium heat, heat the oil and butter. When the foam subsides, add the onion and stir until golden, 5 to 7 minutes. Add the garlic and 2 teaspoons of sirop de Liège. Stir well for about 5 minutes and let it caramelize.

2. Add the vinegar slowly into the mix and deglaze the pan, scraping up any browned bits from the bottom. Allow to boil down for 5 minutes, then sprinkle the flour onto the mixture while stirring. Pour the stock in slowly to blend it in. Add the beer, cloves, thyme, bay leaves, mustard, and the remaining 3 teaspoons of sirop. Stir well. If cooking protein or meat, add it here.

3. Bring to a gentle boil. Cover partially, and simmer on low for an hour, stirring occasionally. Remove the lid, stir well, and add the currants. Simmer uncovered for 20 more minutes, or until it reaches desired smoothness. It should be silky thick.

4. Season with salt and pepper.

STORAGE: *2 weeks in the refrigerator in a glass jar or plastic container, or 4 months in the freezer; freeze it as you would a soup, in a plastic container or silicone reusable freezer bag that can be boiled*

INGREDIENT TIP: *Order sirop de Liège online. Meurens is the best-known brand.*

REPURPOSING TIP: *To use this as a cook-in sauce, brown and pan sear 1 pound of meatballs or cubed beef, rabbit, lamb, or poultry in oil. Add the meat just before Step 3.*

PAIRINGS AND
SERVING IDEAS

MAINS

Stovetop Lamb Loin
Chops (page 147)

Pan-Seared
Crispy-Skin Duck
Breast (page 150)

Turkey Breast
Scaloppini Style
(page 148)

Pan-Seared
Boneless Chicken
Thighs (page 149)

Meatballs

Rabbit

SIDES

Potatoes Four
Ways (page 175)

Bread

Grüne Soße // GREEN HERB SAUCE

GLUTEN FREE • NUT FREE • VEGETARIAN

PREP TIME:
15 MINUTES

MAKES:
ABOUT 1⅔ CUPS

FLAVOR NOTES
TANGY
CREAMY
HERBACEOUS
COOLING

TYPE OF SAUCE
POUR OVER
CONDIMENT

Grüne Soße *is a mix of seven fresh herbs with a dose of cream. Ben Pommer, Head of Culinary at BRLO BRWHOUSE in Berlin, taught me his old Grüne Soße recipe. The sauce is in the same extended family of green sauces as salsa verde, chimichurri, and gremolata, but with added sour cream, yogurt, and, in Chef Pommer's recipe, mustard. Using cream in pesto is a sin in Genovese households (like my mom's), so I cheat by using Grüne Soße when I'm keen for something creamy and herbal. Generally used with boiled veggies, potatoes, and hard-boiled eggs, this sauce is adaptable. Not all the traditional herbs listed here are easily found outside of Germany, so just substitute herbs that are available to you.*

5 cups (about ⅓ pound total) assorted herbs, stemmed and cleaned (pick seven from among chives, chervil, curly-leaf parsley, sorrel, borage, garden cress, tarragon, lemon balm, burnet, dill, and lovage)

¾ cup sour cream or schmand (high-fat sour cream, 20% to 40% fat)

6 tablespoons plain full-fat yogurt

1 teaspoon tarragon or Dijon mustard (see Ingredient tip)

2 tablespoons grapeseed oil

1 shallot, minced

2 teaspoons white balsamic vinegar, plus more for seasoning

Salt

Ground white pepper

1 lemon wedge

SPECIAL EQUIPMENT NEEDED

Food processor

1. In a large food processor, combine the herbs, sour cream, yogurt, mustard, oil, shallot, vinegar, salt, and pepper. Process for about 3 minutes, until finely crushed/puréed.

2. Pass the herb sauce through a mesh sieve into a bowl by pressing the mixture through with the back of a wooden spoon or a spatula. This process takes a couple of minutes as you get all the liquid through (but also doubles as a fun stress reliever).

3. Season with more white balsamic vinegar, salt, pepper, and a spritz of lemon juice to taste.

STORAGE: *3 to 4 days in the refrigerator in a glass container*

INGREDIENT TIP: *To make tarragon mustard, mix equal parts whole-grain or Dijon mustard and chopped fresh tarragon. Season with salt and pepper.*

Senfsauce // MUSTARD SAUCE

GLUTEN FREE • NUT FREE • VEGETARIAN

PREP TIME:
15 MINUTES

COOK TIME:
20 MINUTES

MAKES:
ABOUT 1½ CUPS

FLAVOR NOTES

LUSH

SULFURY

TART

SPICY

HEAT INDEX

TYPE OF SAUCE

POUR OVER
CONDIMENT

*S*enfsauce *is a Bavarian mustard sauce commonly served over boiled eggs and root vegetables.* Eier mit Senfsauce—*eggs with mustard sauce—became a cornerstone of German cuisine in the nineteenth century. The base is a simple hollandaise of butter, lemon juice, vinegar, and egg yolks, with all manner of savory additions. Pair it with fish such as smoked salmon, winter vegetables like broccoli or cauliflower, poultry, or potatoes. Berlin resident Zach Johnston grew up with this sauce and learned it from his mom, who learned it from her German grandmother.*

1 cup vegetable or chicken
   stock (page xv; optional)

1 teaspoon cornstarch
   dissolved in 1½ teaspoons
   water (optional, with
   the stock)

½ pound unsalted butter

Juice of ½ lemon

¼ teaspoon apple cider vinegar

4 large egg yolks

¼ teaspoon ground nutmeg

¼ teaspoon ground allspice

¼ teaspoon paprika

1 teaspoon creamy horseradish

1 tablespoon Dijon mustard

1 tablespoon pickled
   mustard seeds

Salt

Freshly ground black pepper

SPECIAL EQUIPMENT NEEDED

Double boiler or a stainless
   steel mixing bowl set
   over a pot

1. If using stock, gently boil it in a saucepan over medium heat until it reduces to ½ cup, 5 to 10 minutes. Mix in the cornstarch until it thickens to a semi-gelatinous consistency. Set aside.

2. Clarify the butter by heating it in a small skillet over low heat. Skim off the white residue as it arrives at a simmer, until the butter is golden and clear, about 5 minutes. Let cool.

3. Make a simple hollandaise in a double boiler or by bringing a pot of water to a low simmer and placing a stainless steel bowl over it. Add the lemon juice and apple cider vinegar to the bowl, then add the egg yolks while whisking constantly. Continue whisking, and gradually add the warm clarified butter until the mixture becomes thick. If the emulsion breaks, add another egg yolk and mix it again.

4. Add the nutmeg, allspice, paprika, horseradish, mustard, mustard seeds, and stock mixture (if using) as you continually whisk, and season with salt and pepper.

STORAGE: *1 week in the refrigerator in a glass jar or plastic container*

REPURPOSING TIP: *Pour any leftovers over an omelet or poached eggs.*

PAIRINGS AND SERVING IDEAS

MAINS

Sautéed
Thin-Cut Pork
Chops (page 146)

Pan-Seared
Boneless Chicken
Thighs (page 149)

Pan-Roasted
Veggies (page 171)

SIDES

Potatoes Four
Ways (page 175)

Hard-boiled eggs

Rødgrød // SWEET BERRY PORRIDGE

DAIRY FREE • NUT FREE • VEGAN

PREP TIME:
15 MINUTES,
PLUS 1 HOUR TO
MARINATE

COOK TIME:
1 HOUR
30 MINUTES

MAKES:
ABOUT 1 TO
2 CUPS

FLAVOR NOTES
FRUITY
SWEET
SILKY
VIVID

TYPE OF SAUCE
CONDIMENT
GLAZE
SPREAD
MIX IN

There are two versions of Rødgrød—a dessert and a meat sauce. My Danish accomplice, Ole Storm Hansen, recalls eating the dessert version in his grandmother's allotment hut on the outskirts of Copenhagen near the airport during midsummers. In 1655, the Danish king commanded that small gardens be provided on the outskirts of town to help the poor grow their own greens and fruits. Later, in the 1800s, the city's working class used them for the same purpose; the oldest hut still standing traces back to 1821. When I make either version of Rødgrød while barbecuing in my sunny backyard, I'm transported to that Scandinavian countryside paradise, with 747s disrupting the potato gardens. This is the savory version.

⅔ cup sugar

1 cup apple cider vinegar or a tart/sour beer like Mikellers

¾ cup light or fruity beer

1 pound (about 2½ to 3 cups) mixed fresh or thawed forest berries (blackberries, strawberries, raspberries)

2 teaspoons chopped fresh thyme

2 tablespoons potato flour

5 tablespoons water

½ cup lightly whipped cream (optional; omit for Dairy Free / Vegan)

Salt

Freshly ground black pepper

1. Start by making a *gastrik*. In a large saucepan over medium-low heat, heat the sugar just until it starts to caramelize. Do not let it burn or get too dark. Gently pour the vinegar over the sugar. **Do not put your face over the pan as you mix in the liquid,** as it could pop and burn.

2. Do not stir the pot, but allow the liquid to reduce to a thin syrup over medium-low heat, 5 to 10 minutes. The sugar may harden but will eventually reconstitute into a liquid. Add the fruity beer when the sugar is mostly dissolved (it will help dissolve the rest of the sugar) and cook down for another 10 to 15 minutes. Pour the mixture into a dish and set aside to cool; you should have about a cup of syrup.

3. When cool, in a large pot, combine the gastrik and beer mixture and the berries and let sit for 1 hour.

4. Add the thyme, and heat the mixture on low for about 1 hour. The foam should dissipate as it cooks. If it doesn't, cook a little longer until it does. Take the pot off the heat.

5. In a small bowl, combine the flour and water. As soon as the fruit stops bubbling after you take it off the heat, gently add the flour and water (it is very important that the fruit is not boiling when you do this, or the flour will clump), slowly pouring and mixing until a silky *lind* (silky smooth) texture is formed. Stir in the cream (if using).

6. Season with salt and pepper. Pour into a serving bowl and let cool a bit. Serve warm.

STORAGE: *2 weeks in the refrigerator in a glass jar or plastic container, 3 months in the freezer; use small plastic containers and freeze in portion sizes*

REPURPOSING TIP: *To make the dessert version, instead of the gastrik, use 2 cups of elderflower syrup or a liquid sweetener of your choice. Mix the fruit with the syrup and let sit for 1 hour. Then cook over low heat and simmer until the foam dissipates. Take the pot off the heat, then add the combined potato flour and water, and stir until the consistency thickens. Pour into a serving bowl, sprinkle with sugar, and let cool. Serve with whipped cream.*

PAIRINGS AND
SERVING IDEAS

MAINS

Skirt Steak a la
Parrilla (no cream)
(page 144)

Stovetop Lamb
Loin Chops (no
cream) (page 147)

Sautéed
Thin-Cut Pork
Chops (page 146)

Grilled Flanken-
Style Ribs
(page 143)

Pan-Seared
Boneless Chicken
Thighs (no cream)
(page 149)

Pan-Seared
Crispy-Skin Duck
Breast (no cream)
(page 150)

Pan-Seared Sea
Scallops (no cream)
(page 165)

Meatloaf

SIDES

Bell Pepper Egg
Boats (page 172)

Duck Fat Fries
(page 176)

Oven-Baked Potato
Chips (page 175)

Roasted Fingerling
Potatoes (page 177)

Lingonsås // LINGONBERRY SAUCE

NUT FREE

PREP TIME:
15 TO 20 MINUTES

COOK TIME:
1 HOUR

MAKES:
ABOUT 3 TO
4 CUPS

FLAVOR NOTES

TANGY

WINE-LIKE

FLORAL

TART

TYPE OF SAUCE

CONDIMENT

POUR OVER

SPREAD

I n Sweden, winter is Lingonsås season. This recipe comes from Ole Storm Hansen's Swedish mother, who associates it with hunting season. Landowners in Sweden used to receive a jaktkort (quota) to cull the moose herd, based on how much land they owned. If one farmer had a license for 1.3 moose, and their neighbor had one for 0.7 moose, they could combine them to kill two moose and split the meat proportionally. Lingonsås is one of the traditional sauces to pair with cooked moose. The lingonberry is a cousin of the cranberry and red currant. You can substitute either to make this delicious sauce. Use it as a jam for morning toast and pastries. And of course, ditch the canned Thanksgiving cranberry sauce and make this instead.

⅔ cup sugar

1 cup apple cider vinegar or tart/sour beer like Mikellers

⅓ cup veal or stock of choice (page xv)

6 to 8 dried bay leaves

1 tablespoon dry thyme or 1 handful fresh thyme

1 pound (about 2 to 3 cups) fresh lingonberries, cranberries, or red currants (or frozen and thawed; see Ingredient tip)

Salt

Freshly ground black pepper

2½ tablespoons potato flour (or arrowroot powder)

¼ cup water

1 cup heavy (whipping) cream

1. Start by making a *gastrik*. In a saucepan over medium-low heat, heat the sugar just until it begins to caramelize. Do not let it burn or get too dark. Gently pour the vinegar over the sugar. **Do not put your face over the pan as you mix in the liquid,** as it could pop and burn.

2. Do not stir the pot, but allow the liquid to reduce to a thin syrup over medium-low heat, 5 to 10 minutes. The sugar may harden but will eventually reconstitute into a liquid. Pour the mixture into a dish, and set aside to cool.

3. In a large, heavy pan, over medium heat, heat the stock, and add the bay leaves and thyme. Pour in the berries, mix, and cook over medium-low heat for 40 minutes.

4. Pour all of the gastrik over the fruit. Season with salt and pepper. In a separate medium bowl, mix the flour in the water until dissolved. Set aside.

5. Mix the cream into the berry mixture gently, followed by half of the flour and water mixture. Cook for 5 to 10 minutes, until the sauce develops a syrupy consistency. Ideally, when you take a spoonful and turn it upside down, some of the sauce remains on the spoon but most drips off. If you need more of the flour mixture to achieve this, mix in the other half and stir for 2 to 5 minutes.

STORAGE: *1 to 2 months in the refrigerator in a glass jar or plastic container, 4 months in the freezer; use small plastic containers and freeze in portion sizes*

INGREDIENT TIP: *Lingonberries grow in North America, too. You can order them online from a company called Northwest Wild Foods (see Resources on page 200).*

PAIRINGS AND
SERVING IDEAS

MAINS

Grilled
Flanken-Style
Ribs (page 143)

Sautéed
Thin-Cut Pork
Chops (page 146)

Stovetop Lamb Loin
Chops (page 147)

Skirt Steak a la
Parrilla (page 144)

Turkey Breast
Scaloppini Style
(page 148)

Pan-Seared
Boneless Chicken
Thighs (page 149)

Pan-Seared
Crispy-Skin Duck
Breast (page 150)

Sautéed Shrimp
(page 164)

Pan-Seared Sea
Scallops (page 165)

———

SIDES

Bell Pepper Egg
Boats (page 172)

Potatoes Four
Ways (page 175)

Charcuterie board

Cheese plate

Pepparrotsås // NORDIC HORSERADISH SAUCE

GLUTEN FREE • NUT FREE • VEGETARIAN

PREP TIME:
5 MINUTES,
PLUS 20 MINUTES
TO REST

MAKES:
1½ TO 2 CUPS

FLAVOR NOTES

CREAMY

SHARP

TANGY

FRESH

HEAT INDEX

TYPE OF SAUCE

CONDIMENT

MIX IN

Horseradish sauce is a Scandinavian mainstay. This recipe comes from Lisa Karlsson in Norrköping, Sweden. However, similar ingredients and regionally diverse preparations are found in Norway's pepparot saus, Denmark's peberrodssovs, and Finland's piparjuurikastiketta. Horseradish is a classic ingredient in a Swedish smorgasbord. This sauce is ideal for fish, especially of the cured or smoked variety. From there, use your imagination. Pot roasts, any kind of potatoes, red meat, pork, and eggs are all complemented by the sharpness of the horseradish—which in turn is mulled by the smoothness of the crème fraîche. Pepparrotsås is the perfect spread for a roast beef sandwich, or add to ketchup to make a cocktail sauce.

1 cup créme fraîche (see Ingredient tip)

½ cup heavy (whipping) cream, thick whipped

2 teaspoons grated fresh horseradish (see Ingredient tip)

1 teaspoon freshly squeezed lemon juice

½ teaspoon honey

Freshly ground black pepper

Flake salt

1. In a large bowl, mix together the crème fraîche, cream, horseradish, lemon juice, and honey. Let stand for 20 minutes.

2. Add pepper and flake salt to taste and serve.

STORAGE: *4 days in the refrigerator in a glass jar or plastic container; it will get smoother by the day*

INGREDIENT TIP: *Make homemade crème fraîche by combining 1 cup heavy (whipping) cream and 2 tablespoons buttermilk (or sour cream in a pinch) in a jar, screw on the lid, and let sit for 12 to 18 hours at room temperature. Refrigerate until needed.*

INGREDIENT TIP: *Freshly grated horseradish is always best, but in case of emergency, prepared horseradish in a jar or tube will suffice. It is generally half as strong as fresh and significantly less bright.*

REPURPOSING TIP: *If serving the sauce with salad or cold meat (like roast beef), add 1 minced Royal Gala or green apple. If the sauce is to be served with hot meat or fish, add one small finely chopped garlic clove.*

PAIRINGS AND
SERVING IDEAS

MAINS

Skirt Steak a la
Parrilla (page 144)

Sautéed
Thin-Cut Pork
Chops (page 146)

Stovetop Lamb Loin
Chops (page 147)

Wild Salmon Four
Ways (page 155)

White Fish Four
Ways (page 158)

SIDES

Bell Pepper Egg
Boats (page 172)

Potatoes Four
Ways (page 175)

Boiled eggs

Ajika // ZUCCHINI SAUCE

DAIRY FREE • GLUTEN FREE • NUT FREE • VEGAN

PREP TIME:
15 MINUTES

COOK TIME:
45 MINUTES

MAKES:
ABOUT 1⅔ CUPS

FLAVOR NOTES
BRINY
EARTHY
VIVID
ZESTY

HEAT INDEX

TYPE OF SAUCE
CONDIMENT
POUR OVER

There are several types of Ajika, but this is one of the favorites of my close friend Anastasiya Rul, who's Belarusian. Her mother, Larisa, is the kind of European mother who once sent me (a random friend of her daughter) Belarusian socks because she was worried my feet would be cold in the winter. Larisa would make a huge pot of this and store it in canning jars for the wintertime. I was told the kids would forego putting it on the food it was intended for and just eat it right out of the jars.

3 cups (1 pound) zucchini (see Ingredient tip)

1 tablespoon Simple Tomato Sauce (page xiv, or you can use plain tomato paste in a pinch)

2 tablespoons extra-virgin olive oil or sunflower oil

2 tablespoons granulated sugar

1 teaspoon salt

½ teaspoon freshly ground black pepper

½ teaspoon crushed red pepper flakes

7 garlic cloves, minced

4 teaspoons white vinegar

SPECIAL EQUIPMENT NEEDED

Box grater, or food processor grater attachment

1. Grate the zucchini with a box grater on the side with the biggest round holes, or use the grater attachment on your food processor.

2. In a large pot over medium heat, mix the zucchini, Simple Tomato Sauce, oil, sugar, salt, pepper, and red pepper flakes. Bring to a boil, then simmer for 30 to 45 minutes, adding the minced garlic after 25 minutes.

3. Stir in the vinegar at the very end.

4. Use immediately, or store in canning jars.

STORAGE: *2 to 3 weeks in the refrigerator in a glass jar, or years in pressurized canning jars*

INGREDIENT TIP: *If you can find them, use zebra green zucchini or white Russian squash. If not, regular zucchini will work just fine.*

PAIRINGS AND
SERVING IDEAS

MAINS

Sautéed
Thin-Cut Pork
Chops (page 146)

Turkey Breast
Scaloppini Style
(page 148)

Pan-Seared
Boneless Chicken
Thighs (page 149)

Stovetop Mussels
(page 162)

SIDES

Mixed Green
Salad (page 170)

Smashed Garlic Red
Potatoes (page 176)

Fluffy Couscous
(page 181)

Quinoa and Lentils
(page 183)

Black Beans and
Wild Rice (page 186)

PART TWO

USING THE SAUCES FOR EVERYDAY RECIPES

So you've made the sauces. Now what? This part brings the world into your kitchen, showing how you can pair your newfound favorite far-flung sauce recipes with everyday dishes and meals. You'll find simple recipes for meat, poultry, seafood, vegetables, legumes, beans, and grains. For each base recipe, you'll find a suggested sauce or two. Also, every single sauce in the book is paired with one of the recipes in this part, so theoretically you could work your way through this section's suggestions and make every sauce in the book. But hopefully by now, you feel empowered to experiment, explore, and mix and match—choose your own escapade, so to speak.

This section is also the perfect resource when you're looking to repurpose leftover sauces. Running home from work with the knowledge that you have leftover Pesto della Zia in the fridge? You can use it with nearly any of the following base recipes. Combine it with some rice or pasta and veggies, and you'll have an entire delicious meal with extremely minimal effort. Since the recipes in this section were carefully chosen based on both versatility and reusability, this process can be replicated with practically every sauce in the book.

5

MEAT AND POULTRY

Grilled Flanken-Style Ribs

PREP TIME:
5 MINUTES

COOK TIME:
10 MINUTES

SERVES 4

F lanken-style beef spare ribs are a quick, easy weeknight meal. You'll sometimes find them called Korean short ribs. These ribs are typically about a half inch thick and cook quickly over high heat, which keeps them tender and delicious. Use a grill pan, stovetop grill, outdoor grill, or an appliance grill such as a Foreman grill. The flavors of beef hold up well against boldly flavored sauces, such as Gochujang (page 20), Berbere Spiced Sauce (page 98), or Mango Chutney (page 12). Because of the sauce, you don't need much more seasoning than salt and pepper.

2 pounds flanken-style beef spare ribs

1 teaspoon sea salt

¼ teaspoon freshly ground black pepper

1 sauce recipe

Preheat your grill or grill pan to high. Season both sides of the meat with the salt and pepper. Grill the meat for 4 minutes per side, until tender.

GOCHUJANG "SEONG" SAUCE (PAGE 20): *Brush both sides of the ribs with the sauce, and cook for an additional 2 minutes on each side. Serve with more sauce on the side.*

BERBERE SPICED SAUCE (PAGE 98): *Brush both sides of the ribs with the sauce and cook for an additional 1 minute on each side. Serve with more sauce poured over the top.*

MANGO CHUTNEY (PAGE 12): *Remove from the heat, and spoon the sauce over the meat to serve.*

Skirt Steak a la Parrilla

PREP TIME:
10 MINUTES,
PLUS 20 MINUTES
TO REST

COOK TIME:
5 MINUTES

SERVES 4

One of our sins as home cooks is overthinking steak. I've made hundreds of steaks over wood fire coals, and this is still my favorite way to do it. My parrilla partner Jake Williams and I keep it simple by selecting what's known in Argentina as la entraña—*skirt steak*. It's thin so it cooks quickly, and it isn't too expensive. Also, it's fatty and flavorful. Let sauces like Muhammara (page 78), Chimichurri (page 66), and Monkey Gland Sauce (page 102) do the heavy lifting. The meat tastes great on its own.

2 (1-pound) skirt steaks

2 tablespoons coarse-grain sea salt

2 tablespoons freshly ground black pepper

Several pinches crushed red pepper flakes

1 tablespoon clarified butter

1 sauce recipe

1. Season the steaks before cooking by heaping generous amounts of salt and pepper on both sides and letting them rest for about 5 to 10 minutes. Add a pinch of red pepper flakes here and there for a nice surprise.

2. For the parrilla or grill, get your wood coals or 100% hardwood charcoals fiery hot, so the butter singes on the grate, then quickly paint the butter onto the grill. If you're cooking on a stovetop, heat the butter in a large cast iron skillet over high heat until it shimmers.

3. Quickly after buttering the grill or pan, throw on the steaks (you should hear an immediate sizzle) for 3 to 5 minutes, until the bottom is starting to char. Flip and sear on the opposite side for 1 to 2 minutes, until both sides have some char but the meat is pink in the middle. Remove from the heat. Let cool, covered, for 10 minutes before slicing.

MUHAMMARA (PAGE 78): *Serve the steak with the sauce spooned over the top.*

CHIMICHURRI (PAGE 66): *Slather the steak over the top with chimichurri to serve.*

MONKEY GLAND SAUCE (PAGE 102): *Marinate the steaks in half of the Monkey Gland Sauce for about 1 hour before step 1. Then, discard the marinade, wipe off the excess, and cook as instructed. Serve with the reserved half of the sauce ladled over the top.*

Sautéed Thin-Cut Pork Chops

PREP TIME:
5 MINUTES

COOK TIME:
10 MINUTES

SERVES 4

Thin-cut pork chops don't take long to cook, and the pork doesn't tend to dry out, as it does with thicker cuts. This is also an exceptional selection if you're on the go—one of the quickest and easiest recipes here. Pair with rice and serve with a side of Tonkatsu (page 18), Rødgrød (page 130), or the classic accompaniment, Apple Gastrique (page 122).

1 teaspoon sea salt

¼ teaspoon freshly ground black pepper

½ cup flour

Pinch ground cayenne pepper

4 thin-cut pork chops

2 tablespoons canola oil

2 tablespoons unsalted butter

1 sauce recipe

1. In a shallow dish, combine the salt, pepper, flour, and cayenne. Dip the pork chops in the flour mix, coating on both sides. Tap away any excess.

2. In a large skillet over medium-high heat, heat the canola oil and butter until they bubble. Add the pork chops, and cook until browned on both sides, about 3 minutes per side. Transfer to a paper towel–lined plate, and blot away any excess oil.

TONKATSU (PAGE 18): *Serve the pork chops with the sauce spooned over the top.*

RØDGRØD (PAGE 130): *Spoon the sauce over the pork chops to serve.*

APPLE GASTRIQUE (PAGE 122): *Spoon the sauce over the pork chops to serve.*

Stovetop Lamb Loin Chops

PREP TIME:
10 MINUTES,
PLUS
3 TO 8 HOURS
TO MARINATE

COOK TIME:
15 MINUTES

SERVES 4

Lamb loin chops are tender, and they cook relatively quickly. Lamb holds up well against a number of sauces with heavy and strong flavors like Coconut Curry (page 8), Tkemali (page 74), and Sauce Forestière (page 116).

1 teaspoon sea salt

¼ teaspoon freshly ground black pepper

6 garlic cloves, minced

Juice and zest of 1 lemon

1 teaspoon dried oregano

Pinch crushed red pepper flakes

2 tablespoons extra-virgin olive oil

8 lamb loin chops

2 tablespoons canola oil

1 sauce recipe

1. In a small bowl, combine the salt, pepper, garlic, lemon juice and zest, oregano, red pepper flakes, and olive oil. Place the lamb chops in a zip-top bag and add the marinade. Refrigerate for up to 8 hours, but no less than 3 hours. If you don't wish to marinate, then season the lamb chops liberally on each side with salt and pepper.

2. In a large skillet over medium-high heat, heat the canola oil until it shimmers. Remove the lamb chops from the marinade, and pat dry. Working in batches, add the chops to the hot oil. Cook on each side until well browned, 2 to 3 minutes per side.

COCONUT CURRY (PAGE 8): *Pick up the curry recipe at step 3, and continue through to the end of the sauce recipe.*

FOR POUR-OVER SAUCES: *Lower the heat to medium and continue cooking the lamb on one side until the internal temperature reaches 145°F (medium-rare). Tent with foil to keep warm, and rest for 10 minutes before serving.*

TKEMALI (PAGE 74): *Spoon the sauce over the cooked lamb chops to serve.*

SAUCE FORESTIÈRE (PAGE 116): *Pour the sauce generously over the cooked lamb chops to serve.*

Turkey Breast Scaloppini Style

PREP TIME:
10 MINUTES

COOK TIME:
10 MINUTES

SERVES 4

Scaloppini is the perfect weeknight main dish, because pounding the turkey thin means it will cook rather rapidly on the stovetop. You'll need to cook in batches, since pounding the turkey expands it beyond the range of most skillets. To pound, put the turkey between two pieces of kitchen parchment or plastic wrap and whack it with a kitchen mallet.

4 (4-ounce) pieces boneless, skinless turkey breast, pounded thin

½ cup flour

1 teaspoon sea salt

¼ teaspoon freshly ground black pepper

2 tablespoons extra-virgin olive oil

2 tablespoons unsalted butter

1 sauce recipe

1. Pound each piece of turkey to a thickness of one-quarter to half an inch. In a small bowl, mix the flour, salt, and pepper. Dip both sides of the turkey in the flour mix until coated lightly.

2. In a large skillet over medium-high heat, heat the olive oil and butter. Working in batches, cook the turkey in the hot fat until well browned, 2 to 3 minutes per side. Transfer to a plate and tent with foil to keep warm while you prepare the other pieces and any sauce.

LINGONSÅS (PAGE 132) OR SALSA CRIOLLA (PAGE 68): *Serve the turkey with the sauce spooned over the top.*

"CATCH-ALL" BARBECUE SAUCE (PAGE 42): *Use the sauce to add some moisture either by slicing up the turkey and tossing it in a few squirts of the sauce or by using it as a dipping sauce on the side.*

Pan-Seared Boneless Chicken Thighs

PREP TIME:
10 MINUTES

COOK TIME:
10 MINUTES

SERVES 4

*S*kinless, boneless chicken thighs have a slightly heartier flavor than breasts and don't dry out as easily, so they make a really tasty main dish while still serving as an excellent source of lean protein. Chicken thighs also retain and nicely absorb sauces with strong and bold flavors, like Mole (page 56), Jerk (page 54), and Khoresh Fesenjoon (page 82).

8 boneless, skinless chicken thighs

1 teaspoon sea salt

¼ teaspoon freshly ground black pepper

2 tablespoons extra-virgin olive oil

1 sauce recipe

1. Pound each chicken thigh lightly so it is an even thickness. Season with salt and pepper.

2. In a large skillet over medium-high heat, heat the olive oil until it shimmers. Add the thighs and cook until well browned on each side, about 5 minutes on the first side and 6 to 7 minutes on the second side, until the chicken reaches an internal temperature of 165°F.

3. With a slotted spoon, remove the chicken from the pan and set it aside on a platter tented with aluminum foil to keep warm.

MOLE POBLANO DE MI ABUELO (PAGE 56), JERK "STORE" SAUCE (PAGE 54), OR KHORESH FESENJOON (PAGE 82): *Prepare your sauce or add your cooked sauce to the skillet and deglaze the pan, scraping any browned bits from the bottom with the side of a spoon. Bring to a simmer.*

Return the chicken thighs to the sauce, along with any juices that have collected on the platter, and simmer for 1 minute. Turn the thighs, and simmer for 1 minute more.

Serve the thighs with the sauce spooned over the top.

Pan-Seared Crispy-Skin Duck Breast

PREP TIME:
10 MINUTES,
PLUS 20 MINUTES
TO MARINATE
(FOR PONZU)

COOK TIME:
10 MINUTES

SERVES 4

Duck breast is divine. It has flavorful skin that, when properly crisped, is pleasantly resistant, adding an immaculate texture to the duck. Duck can be juicy, lush, or gamey, so I tend to lean toward forthright sauces. Try a drizzle of Ponzu (page 16), or for a hearty accompaniment, use Satay (page 28). Cooking in Sauce Liégeoise (page 124) is certainly recommended here.

4 duck breasts, skin on

1 teaspoon sea salt

¼ teaspoon freshly ground black pepper

2 tablespoons extra-virgin olive oil

1 sauce recipe

1. Preheat the oven to 400°F.

2. Using a sharp knife, score the skin side of the duck breast in a crisscross pattern, cutting down to the meat but not through it. Season the duck breast with the salt and pepper (no salt if using Ponzu).

3. If using Ponzu, place the duck breast skin-side up in a large baking dish, pour on half of the Ponzu, reserving the rest, and marinate for 20 minutes. Remove from the Ponzu and pat dry. Omit the salt. Discard the marinade.

4. For all sauces, in a large skillet over medium-high heat, heat the olive oil until it shimmers. Add the duck breasts, skin-side down, and cook until the fat is rendered and the skin is brown, about 6 minutes. Remove all but about 2 tablespoons of the rendered fat, and flip the duck breasts. (You can use the fat to cook something else, such as potatoes or vegetables, because it is very flavorful.) Cook the duck breast skin-side up until it reaches an internal temperature of 135°F (medium rare), about 4 minutes. Remove from the pan and set aside, tented with foil to keep warm.

PONZU (PAGE 16): *Add the reserved Ponzu to the pan, using the side of a spoon to deglaze the pan, scraping up any browned bits from the bottom. Bring to a simmer, and simmer for 1 minute. Return the duck and any juices that have collected on the platter to the pan. Simmer for 1 minute. Turn the duck once, and simmer for 30 seconds more. Serve with the warmed Ponzu as a dipping sauce.*

SATAY (PAGE 28) OR SAUCE LIÉGEOISE (PAGE 124): *Either prepare the sauce in the same pan as the duck, or heat it in the pan after you've removed the duck, and deglaze the pan, scraping up any brown bits from the bottom with the side of a spoon. Bring to a simmer. Return the duck to the pan along with any juices that have collected on the platter. Simmer for 1 minute. Turn the duck once, and simmer for an additional 30 seconds. Serve with the sauce spooned over the duck.*

6

SEAFOOD

Wild Salmon Four Ways

Wild Salmon is a simple, healthy fish to serve with sauces because it can be cooked in so many ways (farmed salmon can have colorants and carcinogens). Generally, most of the sauces in this book can be poured or spread over your cooked salmon; with others, you may have to coat the fish with the sauce while it cooks. Sauces that go well with salmon include Tomatillo Salsa Verde (page 58), Huckleberry Sauce (page 40), Pepparrotsås (page 134), and Sauvignon Blanc Cream Sauce (page 34).

1 Salmon in Parchment

PREP TIME:
10 MINUTES

COOK TIME:
25 MINUTES

SERVES 4

4 (4- to 6-ounce)
   salmon fillets

Sea salt

Freshly ground
   black pepper

4 tablespoons unsalted
   butter, divided

1 cup dry white wine, divided

1 sauce recipe

**SPECIAL
EQUIPMENT NEEDED**

4 squares kitchen
   parchment paper
   (or aluminum foil)

1. Preheat the oven to 400°F. Lay out four pieces of parchment on a rimmed baking sheet. While the oven preheats, remove any pinbones from the salmon. Using a sharp knife, cut 3 to 4 slits about halfway through the flesh of each fillet.

2. Place one piece of salmon on each piece of parchment, and season with the salt and pepper. Cut each tablespoon of butter into four pieces, and place four butter pieces on top of each piece of salmon.

3. Fold the parchment all around the salmon, leaving it open at the top. Pour ¼ cup of wine into each packet. Close the top of the parchment by folding it over.

4. Bake for 25 minutes, until the salmon flakes easily with a fork.

ALL SAUCES: *Serve the salmon with warm sauce spooned over top.*

2 **Grilled Salmon**

PREP TIME:
10 MINUTES

COOK TIME:
15 MINUTES

SERVES 4

4 (4- to 6-ounce)
 salmon fillets

Sea salt

Freshly ground black pepper

2 tablespoons canola oil

1 sauce recipe

1. Preheat your grill over medium-high heat, or preheat the broiler.

2. Season the salmon with salt and pepper. Dip a paper towel in the oil and, holding it with tongs, liberally oil the grill. Place the salmon flesh-side down on the grill. Cook for 6 minutes. Flip and cook until the internal temperature reads 145°F and the fish flakes easily with a fork, 6 to 8 minutes more. Alternatively, broil skin-side down for 8 to 10 minutes.

SAUVIGNON BLANC CREAM SAUCE (PAGE 34): *Brush the top of the salmon with the cream sauce. Flip and let cook for 1 minute more. Serve with additional sauce spooned over the top.*

TOMATILLO SALSA VERDE (PAGE 58), PEPPARROTSÅS (PAGE 134), OR HUCKLEBERRY SAUCE (PAGE 40): *Serve the salmon with the sauce spooned over the top.*

3 **Baked Salmon**

PREP TIME:
5 MINUTES

COOK TIME:
15 MINUTES

SERVES 4

4 (4- to 6-ounce)
 salmon fillets

Sea salt

Freshly ground black pepper

4 lemon slices

1 sauce recipe

1. Preheat the oven to 400°F.

2. Season the salmon with salt and pepper. Place the salmon filets on a rimmed baking sheet skin-side down, and place a lemon slice on top of each piece of salmon. Bake until the internal temperature reaches 145°F and the fish flakes easily with a fork, about 15 minutes.

SAUVIGNON BLANC CREAM SAUCE (PAGE 34) OR JERK "STORE" SAUCE (PAGE 54): *Remove the lemon slices. Turn the oven to broil. Brush the top of the salmon with the sauce. Broil for 2 minutes on the top rack.*

TOMATILLO SALSA VERDE (PAGE 58), PEPPARROTSÅS (PAGE 134), OR HUCKLEBERRY SAUCE (PAGE 40): *Serve the salmon with the sauce spooned over the top.*

4 Pan-Seared Salmon

PREP TIME:
10 MINUTES

—

COOK TIME:
10 MINUTES

—

SERVES 4

4 (4- to 6-ounce) salmon fillets

Sea salt

Freshly ground black pepper

2 tablespoons unsalted butter

2 tablespoons canola oil

1 sauce recipe

1. Season the salmon with salt and pepper.

2. In a large skillet over medium-high heat, heat the butter and oil until the butter bubbles. Add the salmon, flesh-side down. Cook until golden brown, about 4 minutes. Flip the salmon. Cook until it reaches an internal temperature of 145°F and the fish flakes easily with a fork, 3 to 4 minutes more.

ALL SAUCES: *Serve the salmon with the sauce spooned over the top.*

White Fish Four Ways

White fish is delicate and flaky with a light flavor, so it needs subtle sauces that do not overpower it. Because different white fishes are available regionally, it's best to look for sustainable fish such as (at the time of writing) silver hake, Pacific halibut, sardines, branzino, Atlantic mackerel, many types of trout, char, or barramundi. Cooking times, temperatures, and methods vary depending on the fish size, but working with fillets is pretty standard, so choose whichever of these fish and sauces will work best for you. Suggestions are Yellow Kroeung (page 24), Guasacaca (page 60), Salsa Vizcaína (page 114), and Chermoula Rouge (page 90).

1 White Fish in Parchment

PREP TIME:
10 MINUTES

COOK TIME:
20 MINUTES

SERVES 4

4 (4- to 6-ounce) white fish fillets

Sea salt

Freshly ground black pepper

4 tablespoons unsalted butter, divided

1 cup dry white wine, divided

1 sauce recipe

SPECIAL EQUIPMENT NEEDED

4 squares kitchen parchment paper (or aluminum foil)

1. Preheat the oven to 400°F. Lay out four pieces of parchment on a rimmed baking sheet.

2. Remove any pinbones from the fish. Using a sharp knife, cut 3 to 4 slits in the flesh of each fillet, cutting about halfway down through the flesh.

3. Place one piece of fish on each piece of parchment, and season with the salt and pepper. Cut each tablespoon of butter into four pieces, and place four butter pieces on top of each piece of fish.

4. Fold the parchment all around the fish, leaving it open at the top. Pour ¼ cup of wine into each packet. Close the top of the parchment by folding it over.

5. Bake in the preheated oven for 18 minutes, or until the fish reaches an internal temperature of 130° to 135°F and flakes easily with a fork.

YELLOW KROEUNG (PAGE 24) OR SALSA VIZCAÍNA (PAGE 114): *Remove the fish from the oven, and transfer to the skillet where you are cooking the sauce. Spoon the sauce over the fish and cook, covered, for 5 minutes, flipping the fish halfway through.*

ALL OTHER SAUCES: *Serve the fish with the sauce spooned over top.*

2 Grilled White Fish

PREP TIME:
10 MINUTES

COOK TIME:
10 MINUTES

SERVES 4

4 (4- to 6-ounce) white fish fillets

Sea salt

Freshly ground black pepper

2 tablespoons oil

1 sauce recipe

1. Preheat the grill over medium-high heat, or preheat the broiler.

2. Season the white fish with salt and pepper. Dip a paper towel in the oil and, holding it with tongs, liberally oil the grill. Place the fish flesh-side down on the grill. Cook for 5 minutes. Flip and cook until the internal temperature reads 130°F to 135°F and the fish flakes easily with a fork, 6 to 7 minutes more. If you don't have a grill, broil skin-side down for 5 to 6 minutes until cooked through. If the fish isn't done, flip and cook for 2 to 3 minutes more.

YELLOW KROEUNG (PAGE 24) OR SALSA VIZCAÍNA (PAGE 114): *Transfer the fish to the skillet where you are cooking the sauce. Spoon the sauce over the fish and cook, covered, for 5 minutes, flipping the fish halfway through.*

ALL OTHER SAUCES: *Serve the fish with the sauce spooned over the top.*

3 Baked White Fish

PREP TIME:
5 MINUTES

COOK TIME:
10 MINUTES

SERVES 4

4 (4- to 6-ounce) white
fish fillets

Sea salt

Freshly ground black pepper

4 lemon slices

1 sauce recipe

1. Preheat the oven to 400°F.

2. Season the fish with salt and pepper. Place the fish fillets on a rimmed baking sheet, and place a lemon slice on top of each piece of fish. Bake until the internal temperature reaches 130°F to 135°F and the fish flakes easily with a fork, 10 to 12 minutes.

YELLOW KROEUNG (PAGE 24) OR SALSA VIZCAÍNA (PAGE 114): *Remove the lemon slices, and transfer the fish to the skillet where you are cooking the sauce. Spoon the sauce over the fish and cook, covered, for 5 minutes, flipping the fish halfway through.*

ALL OTHER SAUCES: *Remove the lemon slices, and serve the fish with the sauce spooned over top.*

4 Pan-Seared White Fish

PREP TIME:
10 MINUTES

COOK TIME:
10 MINUTES

SERVES 4

4 (4- to 6-ounce) white
fish fillets

Sea salt

Freshly ground black pepper

2 tablespoons
unsalted butter

2 tablespoons canola oil

1 sauce recipe

1. Season the fish with salt and pepper.

2. In a large skillet over medium-high heat, heat the butter and oil until the butter bubbles. Add the fish flesh-side down. Cook until it turns golden, about 3 minutes. Flip the fish. Cook until it reaches an internal temperature of 130°F to 135°F and flakes easily with a fork, 2 to 4 minutes more.

YELLOW KROEUNG (PAGE 24): *Transfer the fish to the skillet where you are cooking the sauce. Spoon the sauce over the fish and cook, covered, for 5 minutes, flipping the fish halfway through.*

ALL OTHER SAUCES: *Serve the fish with the sauce spooned over the top.*

Stovetop Mussels

PREP TIME:
5 MINUTES

COOK TIME:
15 MINUTES

SERVES 4

Mussels have made my heart sing as my favorite seafood since I was tall enough to see over the counter at my Nonna's. I usually cook mussels on the parrilla with their shells on, but this is her method. It is tried and true. For a sauces book, it has the added advantage of making tiny spoons out of the shells, since she removes half—perfect for lopping up dipping sauces. *Piri Piri Whiskey Sauce (page 118)* is great on any shellfish, but especially mussels because it'll get in all the nooks and crannies of the shellfish.

3 pounds mussels, thoroughly rinsed and debearded

1 stick (¼ pound) unsalted butter

¼ cup extra-virgin olive oil

4 garlic cloves, roughly chopped

1 small handful fresh parsley, chopped, divided

⅓ (1.75-ounce) tube anchovy paste

1 cup dry white wine

Zest and juice of ½ lemon

Sea salt

Freshly ground black pepper

1 sauce recipe

1. In a large, dry, covered pot or Dutch oven over medium heat, heat the mussels until they open—usually about 2 to 4 minutes, but it depends on the mussels. Discard any that don't open. Remove from the heat, and remove the top shell from each.

2. In a large skillet over low heat, melt the butter and heat the oil, then add the garlic and most of the parsley, and sauté for about 5 minutes. Add the anchovy paste, and mix for another minute.

3. Drop the half-shelled mussels into the pan, and mix well.

4. Add the wine and lemon juice and zest, season with salt and pepper, then cook, stirring, uncovered, for an additional 5 minutes. Remove from the heat, and transfer to a large bowl.

PIRI PIRI WHISKEY SAUCE (PAGE 118) AND ALL OTHERS: *Spoon sauce over the top, and mix well. Serve topped with the remaining parsley.*

Sautéed Shrimp

PREP TIME:
15 MINUTES

COOK TIME:
10 MINUTES

SERVES 4

In Louisiana we have two weather seasons and four shellfish seasons: Oyster, crawfish, crab and, of course, shrimp. Gulf shrimp are juicy, puffy, and delicious. Nearly everyone in the state can pontificate on how their recipe or method is the best for shrimp, and I believe every one of them. This is a basic recipe that'll allow the flavor of the shrimp to shine through and not complicate things, so get high-quality shrimp if you can. While Filipino Adobo (page 32) is generally used for chicken, the family recipe in this book is tailored for shrimp, as is the Salsa de Mani (page 62) recipe.

1 pound medium shrimp

½ teaspoon sea salt

¼ teaspoon freshly ground black pepper

2 tablespoons extra-virgin olive oil or unsalted butter

Juice of 1 lemon

1 recipe sauce

ADOBO (PAGE 32): *Add the shrimp as instructed in the recipe, and finish by following that recipe.*

1. Peel and devein the shrimp, and season with salt and pepper.

2. In a large skillet over medium-high heat, heat the olive oil or butter until it shimmers (oil) or bubbles (butter).

3. Add the shrimp and cook, stirring, until they are bright pink and opaque, about 4 minutes. Add the lemon juice and cook, stirring, for 4 minutes more.

SALSA DI MANI (PAGE 62) AND ALL OTHER SAUCES: *Add the sauce to the hot shrimp in the pan. Warm the sauce through before serving.*

Pan-Seared Sea Scallops

PREP TIME:
5 MINUTES
___

COOK TIME:
10 MINUTES
___

SERVES 4

Scallops are like the candy of the sea. They can be sweet, salty, succulent, and fatty. They are a remarkable conduit for drizzled sweet sauces, because of their buttery, savory composition. Yet, for herbal or spicy sauces, they can be oily enough to stand up to the spice. Best of all, they are quick and easy, making them a perfect appetizer while you're preparing other sauces. In that respect, Nam Jim (page 26) is an ideal match because of its tartness, and it can be made a day or two ahead of time.

---

1 pound sea scallops

Sea salt

Freshly ground black pepper

2 tablespoons canola oil or unsalted butter

1 sauce recipe

---

1. Using a sharp knife, trim each scallop to remove the tendon that connects it to the shell. Season your scallops with salt and pepper.

2. In a large skillet over medium-high heat, heat the oil or butter until it shimmers (oil) or bubbles (butter). Add the scallops to the hot fat. Cook until browned on one side, about 2 minutes. Flip and cook until browned on the other side, 2 to 3 minutes more.

3. Using tongs, remove the scallops from the hot fat and set them aside on a platter tented with aluminum foil to keep warm.

NAM JIM (PAGE 26): *Drizzle some of the sauce over the scallops, and set the rest on the side for dipping.*

ALL OTHER SAUCES: *Prepare the sauce in the pan in which you cooked the scallops, and deglaze the pan, scraping up any browned bits that collected on the bottom with the side of a spoon. Return the scallops to the pan, along with any juices that have collected on the platter. Turn once in the sauce to coat. Serve the scallops with the sauce spooned over the top.*

7

VEGETABLES

Vegetable Stir-Fry

PREP TIME:
10 MINUTES,
PLUS 20 MINUTES
TO DRAIN

COOK TIME:
10 MINUTES

SERVES 4

Vegetable Stir-Fry makes a user-friendly vegetarian main dish, or throw a protein in there. Adding chopped tofu or tempeh is always an option as well. My absolute favorite stir-fry sauce is Black Bean Sauce (page 14). Harissa Verte (page 92) can either be added to that or stand alone. My culinary compass points toward Nam Jim (page 26) for its tartness, so go with what you feel—even if it's all three.

1 eggplant, peeled and cut into ½-inch pieces

1 teaspoon sea salt

2 tablespoons canola oil

1 yellow onion, roughly chopped

2 carrots, peeled and roughly chopped

4 ounces shiitake or cremini mushrooms, quartered

6 asparagus stalks, chopped

¼ teaspoon freshly ground black pepper

2 tablespoons Black Bean Sauce (page 14) or Harissa Verte (page 92) or ¼ cup Nam Jim (page 26)

1. In a colander over a bowl, toss the eggplant with the salt. Let rest for 20 minutes for the liquid to come out of the eggplant. Rinse away the salt, and pat dry.

2. In a large, nonstick pan or wok over medium-high heat, heat the oil until it shimmers. Add the onion, carrots, mushrooms, and asparagus, and cook, stirring, until just before they are crisp-tender, about 4 minutes.

BLACK BEAN SAUCE (PAGE 14) OR NAM JIM (PAGE 26): *Season with the pepper, and add the sauce. Cook for an additional 3 minutes, stirring.*

HARISSA VERTE (PAGE 92): *Cook for a minute or 2 more, until the vegetables are crisp-tender. Remove the vegetables from the heat, and toss with the salsa and black pepper before serving.*

Mixed Green Salad

PREP TIME:
15 MINUTES

COOK TIME:
2 MINUTES
(OPTIONAL)

SERVES 4

Catalogued here is the most delightful green salad I've ever had, and I ask for it every time I go back home to Maine. I begged and pleaded with its curator, Lori Austin, to hand it over. She makes it with a simple spicy mustard and maple syrup dressing. Try Pomegranate-Beet Raita (page 6) or thinned Tkemali (page 74) over it, or Hummus bi Tahina (page 86) alongside it.

4 cups organic spring mix (lettuce, spinach, etc.), torn

2 cups mâche rosette, endive, pea shoots, or any specialty leaf, split or torn

1 handful fresh dill, chopped

½ cup halved grapes

½ cup chopped bell pepper

1 tablespoon apple cider vinegar

2 tablespoons pecans (optional)

2 tablespoons extra-virgin olive oil

½ avocado, sliced

3 tablespoons sauce

1. In a large bowl, combine the spring mix, specialty leaf mix, dill, grapes, and bell pepper. Toss with the apple cider vinegar.

2. If using the pecans, lightly toast in a small, dry pan over low heat for 1 to 2 minutes, and add to the salad.

3. Slowly pour on the oil in a thin stream, and top with the avocado slices.

POMEGRANATE-BEET RAITA (PAGE 6) OR HUMMUS BI TAHINA (PAGE 86): *Add a dollop on top.*

TKEMALI (PAGE 74): *Thin with some plum water, and use as a substitute for salad dressing.*

Pan-Roasted Veggies

PREP TIME:
10 MINUTES

COOK TIME:
40 MINUTES

SERVES 4

Pan-Roasted Veggies have a deep, rich flavor that comes from the caramelization of the veggies as they cook on high heat. They make a delicious side dish or a main. Toss the hot vegetables with *Senfsauce (page 128)* or *Romesco (page 112)*. If *you're feeling saucy, dip them in Fondue à la Bière (page 120).*

1 sweet potato, peeled and cut into 1-inch cubes

12 Brussels sprouts, halved

1 red bell pepper, seeds and ribs removed, cut into 1-inch pieces

4 shallots, peeled and quartered

2 tablespoons extra-virgin olive oil

½ teaspoon sea salt

¼ teaspoon freshly ground black pepper

¼ cup sauce

1. Preheat the oven to 400°F.

2. In a large bowl, toss the sweet potato, Brussels sprouts, bell pepper, shallots, olive oil, salt, and pepper. Spread out on two rimmed baking sheets.

3. Roast until the vegetables are soft and browned, 30 to 40 minutes, rotating pans (switching racks) halfway through cooking.

FONDUE À LA BIÈRE (PAGE 120): *Remove the vegetables from the heat. Use skewers to dip them in the fondue.*

ALL OTHER SAUCES: *Toss the hot vegetables with the sauce and serve.*

Bell Pepper Egg Boats

PREP TIME:
5 MINUTES

COOK TIME:
30 MINUTES

SERVES 4 TO 8

*M*arrón con huevo *is a common sight at Argentine parrilladas, which is where I learned the trick from dear friends in Buenos Aires, Guille Maya and Delfina Mansilla. I call them Bell Pepper Egg Boats because that's what they basically look like. They're probably the most popular base at the backyard parrilladas, likely because they are such a good vehicle for holding sauces, bits of bacon, cheese, or anything. Try them with Jajik (page 80), Mojito (page 52), or Chimichurri (page 66)—or any other sauce that has become your favorite.*

4 bell peppers, any color

Extra-virgin olive oil, for oiling the skillet

8 large eggs

1 small (4-ounce) block goat cheese, room temperature, cut into 8 pieces

Salt

Freshly ground black pepper

1 sauce recipe

1. Halve each bell pepper lengthwise, cutting down straight through the top to create two perfectly even "boats." Carefully remove the seeds and ribs without piercing or breaching the flesh.

2. Place the peppers face down (so the boat is upside down) on a large, barely oiled skillet over medium-high heat, and roast until the inside edges of the peppers start to char, 5 to 10 minutes.

3. Flip over the boats, and crack one egg into each; the yolk should remain intact. Cook the boats (covered, if needed) until the egg whites are cooked though and opaque, 15 to 20 minutes. Ideally, the yolks will remain runny.

4. Top each with a piece of goat cheese, and season with salt and pepper. Leave on the heat 1 minute more to slightly melt the cheese.

JAJIK (PAGE 80), MOJITO (PAGE 52), OR CHIMICHURRI (PAGE 66): *Spoon the sauce on top and slather it around before serving.*

Hand-Cut Zucchini Noodles

PREP TIME:
15 MINUTES

COOK TIME:
5 MINUTES

SERVES 4

Zucchini noodles make a harmonious alternative to pasta, and you don't need to have a spiralizer to make your own. All you need is a vegetable peeler and a sharp knife. They are an excellent side dish, topped with excessively flavorful sauces. Think Romesco (page 112), Grüne Soße (page 126), or Tomato "Simba Kali" Sauce (page 100).

4 medium zucchini

2 tablespoons extra-virgin olive oil

Pinch crushed red pepper flakes

½ teaspoon sea salt

¼ teaspoon freshly ground black pepper

1 garlic clove, minced

1 sauce recipe

1. Using a vegetable peeler, cut the zucchini into strips. Then use a sharp knife to cut the strips into half-inch-wide noodles. You can stack the strips and cut through several at once to make cutting go more quickly.

2. In a large skillet over medium-high heat, heat the olive oil until it shimmers. Add the zucchini, red pepper flakes, salt, and pepper. Cook, stirring occasionally, until the zucchini is crisp-tender, about 5 minutes.

3. Add the garlic and cook, stirring constantly, for 30 seconds.

GRÜNE SOßE (PAGE 126): *Remove from the heat and toss with the sauce.*

ROMESCO (PAGE 112) OR TOMATO "SIMBA KALI" SAUCE (PAGE 100): *Add the cooked zucchini to the hot sauce. Cook for 30 seconds to allow the flavors to blend. Serve like pasta.*

Potatoes Four Ways

Can we talk about potatoes? There are so many ways to use them that I could have filled up this entire section with spud versions. I've included four diverse preparations—and any leftovers can be used to make Hand-Rolled Gnocchi (page 187). There are countless combinations with the sauces in this book, but to help dial it in, I've suggested Creole Remoulade and Comeback Sauce (page 46), Grüne Soße (page 126), Fondue à la Bière (page 120), Toum (page 94), Ajika (page 136), Senfsauce (page 128), 'Merican Cheese Sauce (page 44), and Mojito (page 52).

1 Oven-Baked Potato Chips

PREP TIME:
10 MINUTES

COOK TIME:
15 MINUTES

SERVES 4

2 Yukon Gold potatoes, cut into ⅛-inch-thick slices

3 tablespoons extra-virgin olive oil

Pinch ground cayenne pepper

½ teaspoon sea salt

1 recipe sauce

1. Preheat the oven to 400°F.

2. In a large bowl, toss the potatoes with the olive oil and cayenne. Spread in a single layer on two rimmed baking sheets. Roast until the potatoes are crisp, 12 to 15 minutes, rotating pans (switching racks) halfway through cooking.

3. Transfer to a serving plate, and season with the salt.

CREOLE REMOULADE OR COMEBACK SAUCE (PAGE 46) OR GRÜNE SOßE (PAGE 126): *Serve with the sauce on the side as a dip.*

2 Duck Fat Fries

PREP TIME:
10 MINUTES,
PLUS 1 HOUR
TO SOAK
————
COOK TIME:
15 MINUTES
————
SERVES 4

2 medium russet potatoes,
cut into ⅛-inch
matchsticks

4 cups canola oil

2 cups duck fat
(or, for a lighter option,
sunflower oil)

½ teaspoon sea salt

1 recipe sauce

1. In a large bowl of ice water, soak the potatoes for 1 hour, changing the water halfway through.

2. In a large pot or deep fryer over medium-high heat, heat the oil and duck fat until it reaches 375°F.

3. Remove the potatoes from the water, and pat dry with a paper towel.

4. Working in two batches so you don't overcrowd the pot, cook the potatoes in the hot fat until golden brown, 5 to 6 minutes. Remove from the oil with a slotted spoon, and place on a paper towel–lined plate. Blot the excess oil. Season with the salt.

TOUM (PAGE 94) OR FONDUE À LA BIÈRE (PAGE 120): *Serve with the sauce on the side as a dip.*

3 Smashed Garlic Red Potatoes

PREP TIME:
10 MINUTES
————
COOK TIME:
20 MINUTES
————
SERVES 4

1 pound baby red potatoes,
quartered

6 garlic cloves, peeled

¼ cup heavy
(whipping) cream

¼ cup (½ stick) unsalted
butter, cut into pieces

½ teaspoon sea salt

¼ teaspoon freshly ground
black pepper

1 recipe sauce

1. In a large pot, combine the potatoes and garlic cloves, and fill with enough water to cover. Bring to a boil over high heat. Boil until the potatoes are tender, about 15 minutes. Drain in a colander. Return the potatoes and garlic to the pot.

2. Add the cream, butter, salt, and pepper. Using a potato masher, mash the potatoes until roughly smashed. Stir to mix in the butter and cream. Transfer to a serving bowl.

AJIKA (PAGE 136) OR SENFSAUCE (PAGE 128): *Use the back of a spoon to make a crater in the potatoes, and fill it with the sauce.*

4 Roasted Fingerling Potatoes

PREP TIME:
5 MINUTES

———

COOK TIME:
10 MINUTES

———

SERVES 4

1 pound fingerling potatoes, halved lengthwise

2 tablespoons extra-virgin olive oil

½ teaspoon sea salt

¼ teaspoon freshly ground black pepper

2 garlic cloves, minced

2 tablespoons chopped fresh rosemary

1 recipe sauce

1. Preheat the oven to 425°F.

2. In a large bowl, toss the potatoes with the olive oil, salt, pepper, garlic, and rosemary. Spread in a single layer on two rimmed baking sheets.

3. Roast until the potatoes are browned on the outside and tender on the inside, about 10 minutes, rotating pans (switching racks) halfway through cooking.

'MERICAN CHEESE SAUCE (PAGE 44): *Toss with the potatoes before serving.*

MOJITO (PAGE 52): *Lightly spoon over the potatoes, and set some aside for dipping.*

8

LEGUMES, BEANS, AND GRAINS

Fluffy Couscous

PREP TIME:
15 MINUTES

COOK TIME:
15 MINUTES

SERVES 4

Hot couscous is a dreamy main course medium. It's also an ideal cold salad base paired with veggies or mixed with a sauce. Because of the tiny size of the pasta used in couscous, it's astonishingly quick to cook, so using it as a dish when you're in a hurry is still fairly tranquil and unrushed. Combine couscous with a dollop of Haydari (page 76), Cacik (page 76), or Pomegranate-Beet Raita (page 6) as a cold salad, or serve warm with Baba Ghanoush (page 84) or Filfel Chuma (page 88).

FOR THE COUSCOUS

2 tablespoons extra-virgin olive oil

1 shallot, minced

3 garlic cloves, minced

1½ cups unsalted vegetable stock (page xv)

½ teaspoon sea salt

¼ teaspoon freshly ground black pepper

1 cup couscous

FOR THE HAYDARI, CACIK, OR POMEGRANATE-BEET RAITA

1 cucumber, peeled and diced

3 scallions, green parts only, minced

10 cherry tomatoes, quartered

1 cup chopped cooked artichoke hearts

1 recipe sauce

FOR THE FILFEL CHUMA

2 tablespoons sauce

FOR THE BABA GHANOUSH

1 recipe sauce

TO MAKE THE COUSCOUS

1. In a medium pot over medium-high heat, heat the olive oil until it shimmers. Add the shallot and cook, stirring, until soft, about 3 minutes. Add the garlic and cook, stirring constantly, for 30 seconds.

2. Add the stock, salt, and pepper, and bring to a simmer. Stir in the couscous.

3. Turn off the heat. Cover and let sit for 5 to 10 minutes, until the couscous is al dente.

4. Fluff with a fork.

TO MAKE WITH THE HAYDARI, CACIK, OR POMEGRANATE-BEET RAITA

1. Cool the couscous in the refrigerator, and transfer to a serving bowl.

2. Add the cucumber, scallions, cherry tomatoes, and artichoke hearts. Toss to combine.

3. Add the Haydari, Cacik, or Raita, and toss to combine.

TO MAKE WITH THE FILFEL CHUMA OR BABA GHANOUSH

1. Transfer the cooked couscous to a serving bowl.

2. Stir the hot Filfel Chuma or warm Baba Ghanoush into the couscous until well mixed.

Quinoa and Lentils

PREP TIME:
15 MINUTES

COOK TIME:
35 MINUTES

SERVES 6

Lentils and quinoa combine to make a hearty source of protein that's excellent as a main dish or side. It also reheats effortlessly, so it's stress-free to make a batch ahead of time and reheat. You can cook the two in the same pot, as well. Explore serving them in Tikka Masala (page 10) or with Sambel Ulek (page 30) or Zhoug (page 96).

2 tablespoons extra-virgin olive oil

1 onion, chopped

2 carrots, peeled and chopped

2 garlic cloves, minced

4½ cups unsalted vegetable stock (page xv)

1 cup lentils, rinsed

½ cup quinoa, rinsed

1 recipe hot Tikka Masala (page 10) or 1 teaspoon (or more) Zhoug (page 96) or Sambel Ulek (page 30)

1. In a medium pot over medium-high heat, heat the olive oil until it shimmers. Add the onion and carrots and cook, stirring occasionally, until the vegetables are soft, about 5 minutes. Add the garlic, and cook for 1 to 2 minutes more, until fragrant.

2. Add the stock and lentils, and bring to a simmer. Cover and cook, stirring occasionally, for 15 minutes. Add the quinoa and simmer, uncovered, stirring occasionally, for 15 minutes.

TIKKA MASALA (PAGE 10): *Stir in the hot sauce, bring to a simmer, and serve.*

ZHOUG (PAGE 96) OR SAMBEL ULEK (PAGE 30): *Remove from the heat, stir in the sauce, and serve.*

Homemade Pasta Noodles

PREP TIME:
20 MINUTES,
PLUS 10 MINUTES
TO REST

COOK TIME:
3 MINUTES

SERVES 6

Amazing and fresh noodles are fairly easy to make, and I use this recipe from my colleague Alex Bonner. With a pasta roller, you can cut and form them into a variety of shapes and lengths to accompany sauces from all over the world. Ragù della Nonna (wide pappardelle, page 108) or Pesto della Zia (trofie, a short twist, page 110) are my family's classic combinations. But hand-cut noodles also work as cold noodle salads with Chef Nini's Nuoc Mam Cham (angel hair pasta, page 22) or Satay (spaghetti, page 28). For those without a pasta roller, 1 pound of fresh pasta bought from the store will feed about four people.

FOR THE NOODLES

3 cups durum wheat flour

2 tablespoons unfiltered olive oil

1 teaspoon sea salt dissolved in 1 cup lukewarm water

FOR THE SATAY AND NUOC MAM CHAM

½ teaspoon salt

1 recipe Satay (page 28) or Nuoc Mam Cham (page 22)

¼ cup chopped peanuts

2 tablespoons chopped fresh cilantro

2 scallions, green parts only, thinly cut on the bias

Lime wedges

FOR THE PESTO DELLA ZIA AND RAGÙ DELLA NONNA

½ teaspoon salt

1 recipe Pesto della Zia (page 110) or Ragù della Nonna (page 108)

Grated Parmigiano-Reggiano cheese

TO MAKE THE NOODLES

1. In a large bowl or the bowl of a stand mixer, mix together the flour, olive oil, and salt water, and knead either by hand on

a floured surface or with the stand mixer. Continue until you have a soft, workable ball.

2. Let rest for 10 minutes, then knead for 10 more minutes, until the dough is soft and elastic.

3. Roll into ⅛-inch-thick sheets.

TO MAKE WITH SATAY SAUCE OR NUOC MAM CHAM

1. Bring a large pot of water to a boil, and add the salt.

2. Roll and cut the pasta into spaghetti. Add to the boiling water, and cook until al dente, about 2 minutes. Drain.

3. Return the pasta to the empty cooking pot, and stir in the sauce, peanuts, cilantro, and scallions.

4. Serve garnished with the lime wedges.

TO MAKE THE PESTO

1. Bring a large pot of water to a boil, and add the salt.

2. Roll and cut the pasta into 2-inch twists (called trofie), and add to the boiling water. Cook until al dente, 3 to 4 minutes. Drain.

3. Return the pasta to the empty cooking pot, and stir in the pesto.

4. Top each portion with 1 tablespoon of grated Parmigiano-Reggiano and serve.

TO MAKE THE RAGÙ

1. Bring a large pot of water to a boil, and add the salt.

2. In a small saucepan over medium-low heat, warm the ragù.

3. Roll and cut the pasta into thick pappardelle or fettuccine, and add to the boiling water. Cook until al dente, 3 to 4 minutes. Drain.

4. Return the pasta to the empty cooking pot, and add the warm ragù.

5. Top each portion with 1 tablespoon of grated Parmigiano-Reggiano and serve.

Black Beans and Wild Rice

PREP TIME:
20 MINUTES

COOK TIME:
55 MINUTES

SERVES 4

Wild rice takes a while to cook, but it keeps in the refrigerator, so you can cook it ahead of time to save time and reheat when you're in a hurry on a weeknight. Combined with black beans, it's a harmonious, light meal with salsa or sauces like Pebre (page 64), Green Chile "Chacon" (page 48), or Jajik (page 80) to give it a dynamic creamy layer.

2 tablespoons canola oil

1 onion, chopped

1 red bell pepper, ribs and seeds removed, chopped

2 garlic cloves, minced

2¼ cups unsalted vegetable stock (page xv)

1 cup wild rice

½ teaspoon sea salt

1 (14-ounce) can black beans, rinsed and drained

Juice and zest of 1 lime

¼ cup chopped fresh cilantro

¼ cup Pebre (page 64) or ⅓ cup Green Chile "Chacon" (page 48) or 1 recipe Jajik (page 80)

1. In a medium pot over medium-high heat, heat the oil until it shimmers. Add the onion and red bell pepper and cook, stirring occasionally, until the vegetables are soft, about 4 minutes. Add the garlic and cook, stirring constantly, for 30 seconds.

2. Add the stock, rice, and salt. Bring to a boil, stirring. Reduce to a simmer. Cover and cook until the rice is tender, 40 to 45 minutes.

3. Uncover and stir in the black beans. Cook, stirring, until the beans are warmed through, 3 to 4 minutes.

4. Remove from the heat and stir in the lime juice and zest and the cilantro.

PEBRE (PAGE 64) OR GREEN CHILE "CHACON" (PAGE 48): *Stir in the sauce.*

JAJIK (PAGE 80): *Spoon the sauce over the rice, and mix it in roughly with a fork to serve.*

Hand-Rolled Gnocchi

PREP TIME:
20 MINUTES

COOK TIME:
5 MINUTES

SERVES 4

Hand-rolled gnocchi are made with mashed russet (starchy) potatoes and Italian OO flour—a very finely ground flour. In a pinch you can try using your leftover taters from Smashed Garlic Red Potatoes (page 176) or Roasted Fingerling Potatoes (page 177). These gnocchi taste like little cloud pillows, so they nicely complement traditional Italian sauces such as Pesto della Zia (page 110) or Ragù della Nonna (page 108), but are also a strong contender to host things like Butternut-Beet Sauce (page 50). Alternatively, you can try combining these gnocchi with the Tomato "Simba Kali" Sauce (page 100).

1 cup cooked and mashed russet or Idaho potatoes

1 large egg

¼ teaspoon sea salt

1 cup OO flour (more for wetter potatoes), plus extra for rolling

1 sauce recipe

1. In a large bowl, combine the mashed potatoes, egg, and salt. Mix well.

2. Add the flour to the bowl ¼ cup at a time, and mix each addition with your hands until just combined. Sprinkle a little flour onto a baking mat, pastry cloth, or cutting board. Break the dough into four pieces.

3. Roll each piece of dough in the flour (to prevent sticking) and then into a long log or rope about half an inch thick. Cut each rope into half-inch-long pieces.

4. Bring a large pot of water to a boil, and add a pinch of salt. Add the gnocchi to the boiling water, and stir once. Cook until the gnocchi float to the top, about 3 minutes. Drain in a colander.

ALL SAUCES: *Serve topped with the sauce of your choice.*

World Pantry

ITEM	DESCRIPTION	COUNTRY OR REGION	RECIPES
ACHIOTE OIL	A flavored oil made by frying annatto seeds (also called achiote) in oil. Though it doesn't impart all of annatto's earthy flavor, it does turn the oil a golden hue that's perfect for enhancing rice and chicken.	Central and South America Southeast Asia	Salsa de Mani (page 62) Adobo (page 32)
ALLSPICE	Often confused with a spice blend, allspice is a single spice, once mistaken for pepper by early colonizers. It has a musky, clove-like aroma and taste.	Americas	"Catch All" Barbecue Sauce (page 42) Butternut-Beet Sauce (page 50)
BIRD'S EYE CHILES	Extremely hot, thin chile peppers. They're roughly 50k to 100k on the Scoville heat scale.	Southeast Asia	Nuoc Mam Cham (page 22) Sambel Ulek (page 30)
BLUE FENUGREEK	Also called *utsho suneli* and *utskho suneli*, blue fenugreek is an herb. The taste is milder than classic fenugreek seeds.	Georgia Caucasus	Tkemali (page 74)
BRAGG LIQUID AMINOS	A non-GMO, vegan, kosher, and gluten-free substitute for soy sauce and Worcestershire sauce.	United States	Creole Remoulade and Comeback Sauce (page 46)
CASTER SUGAR	Superfine sugar (finer than table sugar but not as fine as powdered or confectioners' sugar) often used in baking. Make it yourself by putting table sugar in the food processor.	Europe	Nam Jim (page 26)

ITEM	DESCRIPTION	COUNTRY OR REGION	RECIPES
COCONUT OIL	An oil extracted from coconuts. It has a relatively low smoke point and contributes a sweet, coconut flavor.	Global	Sambel Ulek (page 30) Coconut Curry (page 8) Jerk "Store" Sauce (page 54)
DASHI (KELP + BONITO FLAKES)	A Japanese stock or broth made from kelp and dried flakes of the bonito fish. It is used to make noodle and soup dishes.	Japan	Ponzu (page 16)
FENUGREEK	A hard, bitter spice from the Eastern Mediterranean. Toasting them develops a sweeter, nutty flavor and aroma.	Eastern Mediterranean Middle East North Africa Europe	Berbere Spiced Sauce (page 98)
FERMENTED BLACK BEANS	Known as *douchi*, fermented black soybeans are used for flavoring stir-fry and soups. They are different from the black beans sold in cans in the supermarket and commonly used in Latin cuisine.	China Japan Southeast Asia	Black Bean Sauce (page 14)
FISH SAUCE	An Asian condiment and liquid sauce base made from fermented and salted krill or fish.	East Asia Southeast Asia	Tonkatsu (page 18) Nuoc Mam Cham (page 22) Yellow Kroeung (page 24) Nam Jim (page 26) Satay (page 28)
FORTIFIED WINE	Brandy or other distilled spirits were added to wine, originally as a preservative. Common ones are port, madeira, marsala, sherry, and vermouth.	Western Europe	Sauce Forestière (page 116) Fondue à la Bière (page 120)
GALANGAL	Also called Thai ginger, a rhizome used widely in Chinese, Thai, and other Southeast Asian cooking.	Southeast Asia China	Yellow Kroeung (page 24)

ITEM	DESCRIPTION	COUNTRY OR REGION	RECIPES
GOCHUJANG	A Korean hot sauce traditionally made by fermenting chile peppers, soybean paste, and rice powder in enormous clay pots.	Korea	Gochujang "Seong" Sauce (page 20)
HATCH AND LEMITAR GREEN CHILES	New Mexico chile peppers are a breed of (usually) green chiles that are hot and light. Hatch and Lemitar are two areas in New Mexico that excel at growing them.	New Mexico	Green Chile "Chacon" (page 48)
HORSERADISH	A spicy root in the same family as mustard and wasabi. It features heavily in the cuisines of Northern Europe and North America.	Europe Western Asia North America	Pepparrotsås (page 134) Senfsauce (page 128)
HUCKLEBERRIES	A berry native to the Pacific Northwest and Western Canada, and a staple of indigenous North American cuisine. Both the black and red varieties are slightly sweet and tart.	North America	Huckleberry Sauce (page 40)
KAFFIR LIME LEAF	A popular ingredient in the cuisines of Southeast Asia and India. They can be used fresh, frozen, or dried and are often deveined and sliced before using.	Asia Indian Subcontinent	Mango Chutney (page 12) Yellow Kroeung (page 24)
LE GRUYÈRE, EMMENTAL, FONTINA, RACLETTE, AND VACHERIN FRIBOURGEOIS	These soft and firm cheeses are ideal for fondue. American Gruyere and Le Gruyère are different. Look for the Swiss +AOP symbol on the labels.	France Switzerland Italy	Fondue à la Bière (page 120)
LEMONGRASS	A citrusy, grassy herb of different varieties used extensively across Asia and Oceania. The tough outer layers should be removed before using.	Asia Oceania Indian Subcontinent	Yellow Kroeung (page 24) Sauvignon Blanc Cream Sauce (page 34)

ITEM	DESCRIPTION	COUNTRY OR REGION	RECIPES
LINGONBERRIES	Native to the Arctic and boreal forests of the northern hemisphere, these berries are a common ingredient in Russian and Nordic dishes. They are a relative of cranberries and feature in Native peoples' cuisine from Canada and Alaska.	Russia Scandinavia North America	Lingonsås (page 132)
MASSAMAN CURRY PASTE	Sweeter and milder than other curries from Thailand and Cambodia. Any mild curry paste will work as a substitute.	Thailand	Satay (page 28)
MIRIN	Sweet rice wine often used to make other sauces in Japanese cuisine. It is similar to sake but generally has a lower alcohol content.	Japan	Black Bean Sauce (page 14) Tonkatsu (page 18)
MSG	A flavor enhancer used to add a salty and umami taste to foods. It can be naturally occurring or processed.	Asia	'Merican Cheese Sauce (page 44)
ÑORA PEPPER AND CHORICERO PEPPERS	The peppers classically used for the dishes of Spain. The ñora pepper is small, round, and has sweet notes. The choricero pepper is the famous Basque variety hung from strings and dried.	Catalonia and Basque Country, Spain	Salsa Vizcaína (page 114) Romesco (page 112)
OYSTER SAUCE	A thick, dark sauce traditionally made by cooking down oysters. Modern methods use thickeners, oyster essences, and flavorings. It is generally added to foods and sauces for an umami enhancer.	China Southeast Asia	Black Bean Sauce (page 14) Tonkatsu (page 18)

ITEM	DESCRIPTION	COUNTRY OR REGION	RECIPES
PALM SUGAR	An unrefined granulated sugar that typically is made by boiling and thickening the sap of palm trees.	Southeast Asia South Asia Africa Middle East	Yellow Kroeung (page 24) Nam Jim (page 26) Sambel Ulek (page 30)
PIRI PIRI PEPPERS	Tremendously hot African chiles that pack an enormous punch. They are up to 175k units on the Scoville scale.	Mozambique Malawi Portugal	Piri Piri Whiskey Sauce (page 118)
POMEGRANATE MOLASSES	Also called pomegranate paste, it is reduced pomegranate juice, used as a tart flavor enhancer in Persia and Assyria.	Middle East Levant Assyria North Africa Indian Subcontinent	Muhammara (page 78) Khoresh Fesenjoon (page 82) Tonkatsu (page 18)
POTATO FLOUR	Made from grinding dried, peeled potatoes. This gluten-free flour holds moisture well. Note that it is not the same as potato starch.	Northern Europe Scandinavia	Lingonsås (page 132) Rødgrød (page 130)
RAMPS	Herbs that most closely resemble spring onions and chives. They are cousins to those plants, and also go by the names wild garlic or wild leek. The European version are called ramsons.	Northern Europe North America	Huckleberry Sauce (page 40)
ROSEBUDS	Used dried in Middle Eastern, North African, Turkish, and Indian cooking to impart flavor and visual delight to a variety of dishes, syrups, and water (rosewater).	North Africa Middle East Indian Subcontinent Turkey Caucasus	Chermoula Rouge (page 90)
SESAME OIL	Oil derived from sesame seeds. It is used primarily to enhance flavor and impart a smokiness in cuisines from Europe to Africa to Asia.	Global	Gochujang "Seong" Sauce (page 20)

ITEM	DESCRIPTION	COUNTRY OR REGION	RECIPES
SIROP DE LIÈGE	This Belgian regional delicacy is made by cooking apples, pears, and dates and then pressing the juice out. It is then concentrated by evaporating most of the liquid.	Belgium	Sauce Liégeoise (page 124)
SMOKED PAPRIKA	Pimentón, as it's also known, is made with different varieties of peppers. The red peppers in pimentón de La Vera are dried only with oak wood at a 5:1 wood-to-pepper ratio.	La Vera and Murcia, Spain	Filfel Chuma (page 88) Hummus bi Tahina (page 86)
SOY SAUCE	An essential ingredient in Asian cuisine, soy sauce is made from fermented soybeans, a roasted grain, and salt.	Asia	Black Bean Sauce (page 14) Tonkatsu (page 18) Ponzu (page 16) Gochujang "Seong" Sauce (page 20) Nam Jim (page 26) Jerk "Store" Sauce (page 54)
STAR ANISE	Considered the national spice of China, star anise has a licorice-like flavor. It is the dried seed of an evergreen tree.	China Southeast Asia Indian Subcontinent	Black Bean Sauce (page 14) Yellow Kroeung (page 24)
SUMAC	Sumac is native to the Mediterranean and has a fruity, citrusy flavor. In Roman times, it was used to sour foods.	Middle East Eastern Mediterranean	Haydari and Cacik (page 76)
SVANETI SALT	Also called Svanuri marili, Svaneti salt is a mixture of salt, dried garlic, and spices from northern Georgia, high in the mountains, near the border with Russia.	Georgia Caucasus	Tkemali (page 74)

ITEM	DESCRIPTION	COUNTRY OR REGION	RECIPES
TAHINI	A sesame paste sometimes thinned with lemon juice and water.	North Africa Middle East Balkans Caucasus	Hummus bi Tahina (page 86) Baba Ghanoush (page 84)
TAMARIND AND TAMARIND CONCENTRATE	Tamarind is the fruit of a tree native to Africa. The pulp is a tangy tart ingredient used in the Middle East, India, Asia, and Europe. The concentrate is made by separating the seeds and refining the pulp.	Middle East Asia Indian Subcontinent Europe	Nam Jim (page 26) Satay (page 28)
TERASI SHRIMP PASTE	This paste is made from fermented shrimp extract and carries an odor to match. Once cooked, it levels out.	Indonesia	Sambel Ulek (page 30)
THAI RED CURRY PASTE	Red curry is called *kaeng pet kat*. It is a fiery red curry that can be made at home or frequently found in the international section of the supermarket.	Thailand	Satay (page 28)
TOMATILLO	Also called husk tomatoes, tomatillos are native to Mexico and Latin America. They are quite hardy and disease resistant. They are more tart and less sweet than tomatoes.	Americas	Tomatillo Salsa Verde (page 58)
YUZU	An aromatic East Asian citrus that is used widely in Japanese cuisine and is common in Korean cuisine to make marmalade.	Japan Korea	Ponzu (page 16)

Measurement Conversions

Volume Equivalents (Liquid)

US STANDARD	US STANDARD (OUNCES)	METRIC (APPROXIMATE)
2 tablespoons	1 fl. oz.	30 mL
¼ cup	2 fl. oz.	60 mL
½ cup	4 fl. oz.	120 mL
1 cup	8 fl. oz.	240 mL
1½ cups	12 fl. oz.	355 mL
2 cups or 1 pint	16 fl. oz.	475 mL
4 cups or 1 quart	32 fl. oz.	1 L
1 gallon	128 fl. oz.	4 L

Oven Temperatures

FAHRENHEIT (F)	CELSIUS (C) (APPROXIMATE)
250°F	120°C
300°F	150°C
325°F	165°C
350°F	180°C
375°F	190°C
400°F	200°C
425°F	220°C
450°F	230°C

Volume Equivalents (Dry)

US STANDARD	METRIC (APPROXIMATE)
⅛ teaspoon	0.5 mL
¼ teaspoon	1 mL
½ teaspoon	2 mL
¾ teaspoon	4 mL
1 teaspoon	5 mL
1 tablespoon	15 mL
¼ cup	59 mL
⅓ cup	79 mL
½ cup	118 mL
⅔ cup	156 mL
¾ cup	177 mL
1 cup	235 mL
2 cups or 1 pint	475 mL
3 cups	700 mL
4 cups or 1 quart	1 L

Weight Equivalents

US STANDARD	METRIC (APPROXIMATE)
½ ounce	15 g
1 ounce	30 g
2 ounces	60 g
4 ounces	115 g
8 ounces	225 g
12 ounces	340 g
16 ounces or 1 pound	455 g

The Dirty Dozen and the Clean Fifteen™

A nonprofit environmental watchdog organization called Environmental Working Group (EWG) looks at data supplied by the US Department of Agriculture (USDA) and the Food and Drug Administration (FDA) about pesticide residues. Each year it compiles a list of the best and worst pesticide loads found in commercial crops. You can use these lists to decide which fruits and vegetables to buy organic to minimize your exposure to pesticides and which produce is considered safe enough to buy conventionally. This does not mean they are pesticide-free, though, so wash these fruits and vegetables thoroughly. The list is updated annually, and you can find it online at EWG.org/FoodNews.

DIRTY DOZEN™

1. strawberries
2. spinach
3. kale
4. nectarines
5. apples
6. grapes
7. peaches
8. cherries
9. pears
10. tomatoes
11. celery
12. potatoes

†Additionally, nearly three-quarters of hot pepper samples contained pesticide residues.

CLEAN FIFTEEN™

1. avocados
2. sweet corn*
3. pineapples
4. sweet peas (frozen)
5. onions
6. papayas*
7. eggplants
8. asparagus
9. kiwis
10. cabbages
11. cauliflower
12. cantaloupes
13. broccoli
14. mushrooms
15. honeydew melons

* A small amount of sweet corn, papaya, and summer squash sold in the United States is produced from genetically modified seeds. Buy organic varieties of these crops if you want to avoid genetically modified produce.

References

Aggarwal, Bharat, with Deborah Yost. *Healing Spices: How to Use 50 Everyday and Exotic Spices to Boost Health and Beat Diseases,* New York: Sterling, 2011.

Atkinson, Catherine, Christine France, and Maggie Mayhew. *The Encyclopedia of Sauces, Pickles and Preserves.* London: Anness Publishing, 2006.

Baljekar, Mridula, Rafi Fernandez, Shehzad Husain and Manisha Kanani. *Complete Indian Cooking: 325 Deliciously Authentic Recipes for the Adventurous Cook.* London: Hermes House, 2004.

Buckley, Marti. *Basque Country: A Culinary Journey Through a Food Lover's Paradise.* New York: Artisan, 2018.

Christensen, Shanti. *Family Style Chinese Cookbook: Authentic Recipes from My Culinary Journey Through China.* Emeryville, California: Rockridge Press, 2016.

Culinary Institute of America. *The Professional Chef: 9th Edition.* Hoboken, New Jersey: John Wiley & Sons, Inc, 2011.

D'silva, Sankhe. *Beyond Curry Indian Cookbook: A Culinary Journey Through India.* Emeryville, California: Rockridge Press, 2016.

Foose, Martha Hall. *Screen Doors and Sweet Tea: Recipes and Tales from a Southern Cook.* New York: Clarkson Potter, 2008.

French, Erin. *The Lost Kitchen: Recipes and a Good Life Found in Freedom, Maine.* New York: Clarkson Potter, 2017.

Gomez, Asha, with Martha Hall Foose. *My Two Souths: Blending the Flavors of India Into a Southern Kitchen.* Philadelphia: Running Press, 2016.

Gramp, D & P. *Mastery of the Sauces: The Culinary Library, Volume 3.* CreateSpace Independent Publishing Platform, 2014.

Hernandez, Eddie, and Susan Puckett. *Turnip Greens and Tortillas: A Mexican Chef Spices Up the Southern Kitchen.* New York: Houghton Mifflin Harcourt, 2018.

Lakshmi, Padma, with Judith Sutton and Kalustyan's. *Encyclopedia of Spices and Herbs.* New York: Ecco Press, 2016.

Mallmann, Francis. *On Fire: 100 Inspired Recipes to Grill Anywhere, Anytime.* New York: Artisan, 2014.

Moore, Matt. *The South's Best Butts: Pitmaster Secrets for Southern Barbecue Perfection.* New York: Oxmoor House, 2017.

Ortiz, Elisabeth Lambert. *The Encyclopedia of Herbs, Spices and Flavorings: A Cook's Compendium.* New York: Dorling Kindersley, 1992.

Page, Karen, and Andrew Dornenburg. *The Flavor Bible: The Essential Guide to Culinary Creativity, Based on the Wisdom of America's Most Imaginative Chefs.* New York: Little, Brown & Company, 2008.

Parisi, Grace. *Get Saucy: Make Dinner a New Way Every Day with Simple Sauces, Marinades, Dressings, Glazes, Pestos, Pasta Sauces, Salsas, and More.* Cambridge, Massachusetts: Harvard Common Press, 2005.

Sercarz, Lior Lev. *The Spice Companion: A Guide to the World of Spices.* New York: Clarkson Potter, 2016.

Seder, Vanessa. *Secret Sauces: Fresh and Modern Recipes with Hundreds of Ideas for Elevating Everyday Dishes.* London: Kyle Books, 2017.

Sheraton, Mimi. *1000 Foods to Eat Before You Die: A Food Lover's Life List.* New York: Workman Publishing Company, 2014.

Sherman, Sean, with Beth Dooley. *The Sioux Chef's Indigenous Kitchen.* Minneapolis, Minnesota: University of Minnesota Press, 2017.

Stevens, Mark. *Cooking With Spices: 100 Recipes for Blends, Marinades, and Sauces from Around the World.* Emeryville, California: Rockridge Press, 2017.

Turshen, Julia. *Now and Again: Go-To Recipes, Inspired Menus and Endless Ideas for Reinventing Leftovers.* San Francisco: Chronicle Books, 2018.

Williams, Sallie Y. *The Complete Book of Sauces: Recipes for More Than 300 Sauces and Dressings for Poultry, Meat, Fish, Pasta, Salads, Vegetables, and Desserts.* New York: Houghton Mifflin Harcourt, 1990.

Resources

FOOD BLOGS AND RECIPES

BEETZEATS
Beeta Mohajeri's website, with tantalizing recipes from around the world
BeetzEats.com

BLANK PALATE
Marti Buckley's blog about living and eating in Basque Country, Spain. Her Book, Basque Country, *is an essential resource for understanding Basque cuisine and culture.*
TravelCookEat.com

CARDAMOM AND TEA
Kathryn Pauline's outstanding Assyrian-inspired food blog
CardamomAndTea.com

THE INTERNATIONAL TABLE
Recipes from all over with photos that will make you want to lick your screen
HatzfeldCreative.com /the-international-table

SERIOUS EATS
Food, recipes, podcasts . . . everything
SeriousEats.com

THE SIOUX CHEF
Sean Sherman is leading the way in the Indigenous Food Movement. The Sioux Chef Cookbook is a must-own.
Sioux-Chef.com

YAZZIE THE CHEF
Brian Yazzie is a chef from the Navajo Nation and writes about North American indigenous foods (click on the "Press" section).
YazzieTheChef.com

GROCERIES AND MARKETS

AMIGO FOODS
Latin American products and foods, including yerba maté, broken down by country
AmigoFoods.com

ASIAN FOOD GROCER
Asian groceries, tableware, and even toys
AsianFoodGrocer.com

BELGIAN SHOP
A great source for beer, chocolate, waffles, and cheeses from Belgium
BelgianShop.com

FOODS IN SEASON
Purveyors of fresh wild foods delivered overnight
FoodsInSeason.com

KALUSTYAN'S
Salts, spices, snacks, sweets, syrups, sauces, seasonings and many other items from around the world
FoodsOfNations.com

LA TIENDA
Just about every food product from Spain you can imagine, including cheese, ham, and pantry staples
Tienda.com

LOCAL HARVEST
A list of local farmers' markets and CSAs
LocalHarvest.org

NORTHWEST WILD FOODS
Dried and frozen berries, smoked seafood, mushrooms, nuts, and wonderful fruit powders, all from North America
NWWildFoods.com

RED STICK SPICE CO.
Salts, peppers, oils, and vinegars, and some interesting recipes, too
RedStickSpice.com

ROYAL MERCHANT TRADING CO.
High quality spices sourced ethically, with the origin printed on each bag
RoyalMerchant.co

THE SPICE AND TEA EXCHANGE
Spice, tea, salts, sugars, and blends of all those things
SpiceAndTea.com

KITCHEN TOOLS AND COOKWARE

STAUB

Cast iron cookware, including Dutch ovens, cocottes, and saucepans
Staub-Online.com

ZWILLING

Top-quality saucepans, knives, cookware, and kitchen tools
Zwilling.com

Sauces Index

Index

Acknowledgments

Jess Kearney, I couldn't ask for a better travel or food consumption partner. Thank you for your unwavering support and patience during this process. I love you.

David Stevens and Lori Austin, thank you for teaching me accountability and discipline and for the ability to compartmentalize and objectively find solutions.

Maria Cristina and Rick Stephenson, thank you for giving me the tools to be a respectful and insatiably curious traveler.

Nonna Yvelise, *ti voglio un gran bene, sempre. Voglio che tu sia sempre orgogliosa di me. Tu e il Nonno siete nel mio cuore.*

Zia Elda, *sono contento che sei nella mia vita. I tuoi viaggi mi hanno dato ispirazione. Ti voglio bene.*

Simon, Corie, Samantha, and Amelia, may this book play the smallest of parts in making the world a smaller, more accessible place.

Carla Roncoli and Tom Painter, your great example of taking interest in the places and people near and far is instrumental in endeavors such as this. Thank you.

Beeta Mohajeri, once again you've made the case for a book of your own. I hope to one day contribute to that masterpiece.

Jeanie Laksmi, thank you for being generous with your time, patient with my questions, and sensitive to my chile pepper tolerance.

Alyssa Lamrawee Hanpongpandh, you are a master of your craft. Everyone headed to Thailand should visit Food and Arts by Alyssa to learn more about Thai cuisine.

Zanzuki and Satomi were instrumental in their advice on Japanese food. *Arigato.* I genuinely feel sorry for everyone who visits Tokyo and doesn't get to hang out with them.

Chris LeBlanc, you are number one. Your face is number one. Your remoulade is number one.

Jack Hatzfeld and James Kihara Munuhe, I look forward to watching as you conquer the culinary and travel worlds.

I am overjoyed to have Tanny Jiraprapasuke and her mom, Kanya, in print.

Chef Seong Hwang, you didn't have to take a break from cooking for my favorite athletes to send me a recipe, but I'm so glad you did. Thank you, Chef.

Sonali Fernando, I appreciate you more than you know. Thank you for your counsel both on food and life.

Going to Siem Reap? Let Lin guide you. You'll make a friend for life. Shayne Tingle, thank you for the connection!

Chef Nini Nguyen, you make New Orleans proud! Thank you for providing your family recipe! Readers: Follow her immediately and you'll be on a rocket shooting to the moon.

To the Chacon family for your coveted green chile, thank you.

Gratitude would not be complete without my UPROXX family: Brett Michael Dykes, Steve Bramucci, Vincent Mancini, and especially the wisdom of Zach Johnston.

Allison Sanchez and Lisa Dunn, this book is better because of hamroom. Mostly because of y'all. But also because ham. Thank you for embracing my weirdness.

It is my absolute honor to know Brian Yazzie. Watch for him. You'll be able to say you knew about him when. . . .

Gracias, **Marcelo Panta (y Sarah Jean Couture),** *gracias por tu ayuda!*

Lucas "Petry" Fernández Díaz (y Guille Maya), *gracias flacos, nos vemos in Buenos Aires!*

Carolina Moppett, you have made me an unofficial footy fan of Uruguay*Fuerza!*

Raquel Vadia and Danny Muñoz, Lucas and Lila, *gracias, cariños por todo, siempre.*

José Manuel Simián, thank you for being first off the line to help a stranger. Here's to a new lifelong friend.

Lola Lozano, *Papa Lara estaría feliz espero. Usé pimientos rojos picantes. Te quiero bien siempre.*

Marti Buckley, thank you so much for contributing. It is a huge honor to include you. Until the next pintxos in San Sebastian. . . .

Manuel Banazol, I'm ecstatic for you, Papa Banazol! These years have been kind to you, my friend.

Nicks: Travis, Two-Shack and Denver, you bloody beautiful legends. Thanks for being on the ride.

Camille De Gend, *merci beaucoup!* I'm so thrilled for you to be here and happy.

Bron Moyi, congratulations on e'rything, my friend. And thank you for your help and consideration.

Ben Pommer, thank you for your willingness to help a stranger. See you at BRLO.

Ole Storm Hansen, you officially have the coolest name of anyone I've ever met and I'm so looking forward to steaks and sauces in Denmark.

Lisa Karlsson, you swooped in and saved my bacon. Thank you!

Anastasiya Rul, to one of my favorite humans. Thank you for always being there when I needed you. This time is no different. I couldn't imagine someone better prepared to be an outstanding, caring mother. Congratulations!

Margarita Gerliani, you are a gem. Thank you for contributing to this project. Recipes like Tkemali, straight from the Svaneti, are what make this book special.

Raja Maatar and Dar Souad, I hope to see this book in the restaurant in Tunis!

Kathryn Pauline, thank you for jumping aboard with enthusiasm. I can't wait to follow you as your book takes off!

TJ Jawad Trad, the pride you get when speaking about toum is the pride I want for everything, but have yet to achieve. Thank you!

Yolandé van Heerden, monkey glands are my treat next time! Thank you for your love and friendship.

Thank you to the one and only Matt Moore, Barbecue Legend!

Willy Trullas Moreno, for your help deciphering the difference between Romesco and Salvitxada, after an exhaustive search.

Suzie Abdou, Erene Mina, and Maryanne Wageh Guirguis, for your contributions . . . and for diving in the deep end with me, a stranger. This scenario is the heart of this book. Thank you.

Joe McReynolds and Fabienne Gray, thank you for never letting the wine supply ever really reach empty.

Alex Bonner, for jumping aboard once again!

Paul Rahfield and Tara Tomasiewicz, as always, thank you for unlimited use of your culinary knowledge and resources . . . and booze.

Thank you Jake and Rachel Williams for always being ready to fire up the parrilla.

To Beril Guceri and her mom, Semra, and Shawn Bunkheila and his dad, Ghazi, for last-minute familial accuracy checks. Thank you so much.

Jon Mallard, for setting me on this path.

Martha Foose, I often wonder why and how I get to have you as a friend and mentor. So much love to you, your family, and the good people of Pluto and Greenwood.

To my editor, Kim Suarez, thank you for your guidance, patience, and for making this experience a team effort. Travel cookbooks exist! Onward.

Susan Puckett, it has been my absolute pleasure to know you and be a recipient of your knowledge and kindness. Thank you for embracing my weirdness with open arms.

Aric S. Queen, this book literally and literarily wouldn't exist without your help and enthusiastic championing. Thank you so much, wherever you are.

To the Dream Brothers, dream on.

And Shareen Chehade and Sharree Walls, in remembrance.

About the Author

MARK C. STEVENS is a native of Maine and a dual citizen of the United States and Italy. He is an internationally published food writer, experiential traveler, and avid home cook. In 2017, while writing his first cookbook, Mark combined his love affairs with travel and food by completing the Continent Grand Slam: visiting all seven continents in a calendar year. In 2018, he completed the fifty US States and the District of Columbia. When home, he is generally occupied with hosting *parrilladas*—Patagonian wood-fire barbecues he learned in Bariloche, Argentina—at his house in the Fairgrounds neighborhood of New Orleans. Mark also works in movies and TV. Now a Directors Guild of America First Assistant Director, his past credits include *Beasts of No Nation*, *Lemonade*, and *Dallas Buyers Club*. His first book is *Cooking with Spices: 100 Recipes for Blends, Marinades, and Sauces from Around the World*, published in 2017. He has lived in New Orleans since 2008.

CPSIA information can be obtained
at www.ICGtesting.com
Printed in the USA
JSHW050301031220
9974JS00005B/10